Vegetable frittata from the pressure cooker

Servings: 2
Preparation time: 30 minutes

Ingredients:

1 clove of garlic, crushed
1 onion, diced
1 potato, diced
1 courgette, finely chopped
1 pinch of salt
1 pinch of pepper
1 tbsp olive oil for the rice cooker or pressure cooker
1 tbsp oil for the frying pan
6 eggs, beaten
2 tbsp grated cheese of your choice

Preparation:

1. Heat oil in a frying pan.
2. Add the garlic clove and sweat briefly so that the bitter aroma can develop. Then remove so that the dish does not become too bitter later.
3. Add the vegetables to the pan. Sweat for 1-2 minutes over low heat. Season with salt and pepper. Then remove from the heat.
4. Pour olive oil into the rice cooker or pressure cooker and drizzle it on the inside.
5. Add all the ingredients, mix and cook on standard settings - for the saucepan: cook for 15 minutes.
6. Done. Stir and serve.

Steamed potato wedges

Servings: 4
Preparation time: 20 minutes

Ingredients:

750 g potatoes, floury, cut into potato wedges
250 ml vegetable stock
1 pinch paprika powder
1 tsp garlic powder
½ tsp onion powder
4 tbsp olive oil
1 pinch of pepper
1 pinch of salt

Preparation:

1. Heat the olive oil in a saucepan.
2. When the oil is hot, add the potatoes and cook for 6 minutes.
3. Add the rest of the ingredients and mix well.
4. Close the lid and cook for 6 minutes.
5. Open the lid with the cold water method.
6. Serve hot and enjoy.

Vegetable curry with chickpeas and pumpkin

Servings: 6

Preparation time: 6 hours 10 minutes

Ingredients:

200 g chickpeas, soaked
300 g pumpkin, diced
1 tbsp garlic powder
1 tsp chilli powder
1 tbsp cumin powder
500 ml vegetable stock
70 g cabbage, chopped
500 ml coconut milk
3 garlic cloves, crushed
1 onion, diced
3 tbsp olive oil
1 tsp pepper

Preparation:

1. Put ingredients in saucepan and mix well.
2. Close lid and simmer on low heat for 6 hours.
3. Serve warm. Serve with rice.

Coconut vegetable curry

Servings: 2
Preparation time: 15 minutes

Ingredients:

250 ml vegetable stock
250 ml coconut milk
1 tbsp curry paste
1 tsp ginger
1 pinch of salt
170 g pepper, chopped
100 g green beans
2 carrots, diced
1 sweet potato, diced
150 g tofu, diced
1 tbsp lemon juice
1 tbsp basil, chopped

Preparation:

1. Put vegetable stock, coconut milk, ginger, salt as well as curry in saucepan. Bring to the boil. Once boiling, add peppers, beans, carrots and potatoes.
2. Simmer on low heat for about 5 minutes.
3. Add the tofu and simmer for another 5 minutes.
4. Season with the remaining ingredients, stir and serve. Enjoy hot.

Cucumber-Fennel Smoothie

Servings: 2
Preparation time: 10 minutes
Prepare dish only starting from the 3-4th week of the diet!

Ingredients:

½ fennel
1 large cucumber
2 cm piece of ginger
1/2 tablespoon lemon juice
2 Granny Smith apples
4 stalks of celery

Preparation:

1. First blend the celery stalks piece by piece in the blender.
2. Then blend the remaining ingredients as well.
3. Mix everything together and serve.

Kale tabbouleh

Servings: 3
Preparation time: 15 minutes
Do not prepare dish until 3-4 weeks of diet!

Ingredients:

Lettuce:
2 bunches parsley, chopped
100 g kale, de-stemmed
30 g fresh mint leaves, chopped
300 g cherry tomatoes, halved
150 g cucumber, diced
150 g hemp seeds
70 g spring onions, diced

Dressing:
200 ml olive oil
120 ml lemon juice
2 cloves garlic, crushed
2 tablespoons spring onions, finely diced
1 teaspoon sea salt
1 teaspoon thyme
1 teaspoon black pepper

Preparation:

1. **Salad:** Chop the de-stemmed and washed kale and place in a bowl. Salt. Use your hands to massage the salt evenly into the kale until it becomes wilted and soft.
2. Add the chopped parsley and mint to the bowl. Mix well.
3. Add remaining salad ingredients and mix.
4. **Dressing:** blend all dressing ingredients except olive oil in a blender. Gradually add the olive oil while blending.
5. Place the salad on plates and drizzle with the dressing.
6. Serve and enjoy.

Quinoa-Almond Salad

Servings: 2
Preparation time: 30 minutes

Ingredients:

3 tablespoons almonds
40 g quinoa
130 ml water
2 teaspoons olive oil
1/2 yellow pepper, diced
1 clove garlic, crushed
1 spring onion, thinly sliced
A pinch of red pepper flakes
1 teaspoon thyme
1/2 medium courgette, diced
1/2 large celery stalk, diced
Juice of half a lime
Salt and pepper to taste

Preparation:

1. Preheat the oven to 180°C. Place the almonds on a baking tray (preferably lined with baking paper) and toast in the oven until crisp and lightly fragrant. Preparation time approx. 7 minutes. Remove from the oven and set aside.
2. Heat 1 teaspoon olive oil in a saucepan over medium heat. Add the peppers, garlic, spring onions and red pepper flakes. Stir and fry for about 5 minutes. The pepper pieces should have softened nicely.
3. Stir in the quinoa, thyme, water and a pinch of salt. Now bring to the boil and then simmer for 7 minutes.
4. Stir in the courgettes. Cover and simmer until the quinoa is tender but not mushy. Should take about 5-8 minutes. Remove pot from heat.
5. Add the celery, almonds and remaining olive oil. Salt and season, then use a fork to fluff up the dish. Serve warm or cold - season with lime juice when serving.

Paprika Bean Puree with Oregano

Servings: 4
Preparation time: 40 minutes

Ingredients:

200 g pinto beans, rinsed
½ tsp cumin
1 tsp oregano
500 ml water
500 ml vegetable stock
½ jalapeño, in pieces
2 cloves of garlic, crushed
½ onion, diced
½ tbsp olive oil
1 pinch of salt
1 pinch of pepper

Preparation:

1. Heat the olive oil in a saucepan.
2. When hot, sauté the onions, jalapeño and garlic.
3. Add the rest of the ingredients and mix well.
4. Close the lid of the pressure cooker and cook for 30 minutes.
5. Allow the pressure to release normally.
6. Mash the bean mixture in a bowl.
7. Season with salt and pepper.
8. Serve warm and enjoy.

Lentil stew

Servings: 4
Preparation time: 25 minutes

Ingredients:

1 onion, diced
2 tbsp olive oil
1 tsp ginger
2 cloves garlic, crushed
½ tsp turmeric
1 tbsp basil
200 g lentils
750 ml water
1 pinch of salt
A little parsley for decoration

Preparation:

1. Fry the onions. Then add olive oil with ginger, garlic, turmeric and basil. Sauté over a low heat.
2. Add the lentils. Sauté. Heat water and add to lentil mixture. Close the lid and bring to the boil.
3. Then simmer on low heat for 15 minutes. Stir regularly and add salt.
4. Serve and garnish with parsley.

Arugula Sweet Potato Salad

Servings: 4

Preparation time: 15 minutes or 3 hours 15 minutes respectively.

Ingredients:

400 g sweet potatoes, boiled, diced
100 g bean sprouts
2 red peppers, chopped
1 onion, diced
A few arugula leaves
30 g almonds
120 ml mayonnaise (sugar-free)
Juice of one lemon
2 tbsp olive oil
1 pinch of pepper
1 pinch of salt

Preparation:

1. Mix the ingredients in a salad bowl.
2. Add mayo, olive oil, lemon juice and seasoning.
3. Mix well and leave in the fridge for three hours.
4. Serve and enjoy.

Kidney bean stew

Servings: 4
Preparation time: 60 minutes
Do not prepare dish until 3-4 weeks of diet!

Ingredients:

2 tbsp olive oil
2 vegetable stock cubes, crumbled
2 onions, diced
2 apples, peeled and cored (variety: Granny Smith)
2 carrots, peeled
3 tbsp tomato puree (without additives, sugar-free)
250 ml water
1 tsp oregano
1 tsp caraway
300 g kidney beans, pre-cooked
1 pinch of salt
1 pinch of pepper

Preparation:

1. Preheat oven to 180 degrees. Sauté onions, vegetable stock, apples and carrots for five minutes, stirring constantly in olive oil.
2. Mix the water with the tomato paste. Add to the sautéed mixture together with oregano and cumin. Mix well. Simmer for 2 minutes.
3. Add the remaining ingredients and pour the mixture into the casserole dish. Cover and bake in the oven for 40 minutes.
4. Serve hot and enjoy.

Pumpkin soup with beetroot

Servings: 4
Preparation time: 60 minutes

Ingredients:

30 ml coconut oil
2 onions - chopped
1 pumpkin (butternut or pear squash respectively)
800 g beetroot - Peeled, chopped, cooked
450 g sweet potatoes - Peeled, diced
300 g leek - finely chopped
2 cloves garlic - crushed
1 teaspoon with cinnamon
1 litre stock (chicken or vegetable)
1 pinch of nutmeg
2 cm piece of ginger - peeled, chopped
1 pinch of salt
1 pinch of pepper
A little coriander - chopped

Preparation:

1. Fry onions, ginger and garlic for 3 minutes over medium heat.
2. Add the leeks and stir well for 5 minutes.
3. Add the pumpkin, beetroot and sweet potato. Deglaze with the stock.
4. Add the cinnamon, salt, pepper and nutmeg. Stir.
5. Bring to the boil, cover and simmer for 30-40 minutes until the vegetables are tender.
6. Stir in the chopped coriander and chilli flakes.

Cauliflower Muffins with Broccoli

Servings: 1 muffin tin
Preparation time: 40 minutes
Do not prepare dish until the 3-4th week of the diet!

Ingredients:

70 g cauliflower, cooked
70 g broccoli
40 g cheese, grated
1 teaspoon mustard (absolutely sugar-free, without additives)
5 eggs
1 tsp coconut oil, melted
1 pinch of salt
1 pinch of pepper

Preparation:

1. Preheat the oven to 180°C.
2. Grease the muffin tin with the coconut oil.
3. Place the cooked cauliflower and broccoli in the muffin tin.
4. Whisk together the eggs, mustard, cheese, coconut oil, salt and pepper.
5. Pour equal amounts of everything into the mould.
6. Place in the oven and bake for 25 minutes.
7. Leave to cool for 5 minutes.

Pumpkin juice with vegetables

Servings: 7
Preparation time: 20 minutes

Ingredients:

4 carrots
200 g cabbage
100 g fresh chives
350 g broccoli florets
450 g pumpkin (diced)
220 g radish
1 litre coconut water
2 onions
4 cloves of garlic
A few ice cubes
A pinch of salt and pepper

Preparation:

1. Place cabbage leaves in ice water.
2. Peel and chop the remaining ingredients (if applicable).
3. Wash broccoli thoroughly.
4. Juice the ingredients in the juicer.
5. Add the coconut water and mix.
6. Season with salt and pepper.
7. Serve garnished with radish slices.

Cauliflower soup

Servings: 4
Preparation time: 120 minutes

Ingredients:

1 large head of cauliflower
5 garlic cloves, peeled
1 red onion, finely diced
1 tsp paprika powder
1 tsp sea salt
1 tsp black pepper
1 litre vegetable stock
4 tbsp olive oil

Preparation:

1. Preheat the oven to 180°C.
2. Place the whole head of cauliflower on a baking tray in the oven with the oil, salt, paprika, garlic and black pepper.
3. Bake for 1 ½ hours with 120 ml of water in the baking tray, or until you can easily pierce the centre of the cauliflower with a knife.
4. Roughly chop the cauliflower after letting it cool for a few minutes.
5. Heat the olive oil in a large saucepan over a medium heat and add the onions, sweat until just translucent. This will take 2 - 3 minutes to prepare.
6. Add the chopped cauliflower and vegetable stock to the pot.
7. Bring the mixture to a simmer in the pot over medium-low heat, cooking until the cauliflower is tender. This should take about 10 minutes to prepare.
8. Pour the mixture into a food processor and puree in small batches until completely smooth, like a soup.
9. Pour back into the pot, bring the soup back to a simmer before serving.
10. Serve hot.

Cauliflower puree with cheese and bacon

Servings: 6
Preparation time: 35 minutes

Ingredients:

1 head of cauliflower
1 tsp salt
1 tsp pepper
5 slices bacon
60 g cream cheese
75 g cheddar

Preparation:

1. Preheat the oven to 180°C.
2. Fry the bacon in a pan and chop it.
3. Wash the cauliflower, remove the leaves and chop the cabbage.
4. Bring a pot of water to the boil and add the cauliflower, cook for nine minutes.
5. Dice the cheese.
6. Drain the cauliflower.
7. Mash the cream cheese and cauliflower together.
8. Season with pepper and salt.
9. Add the bacon and cheese.
10. Place in the casserole dish and put in the oven.
11. Bake for 10 minutes.
12. Remove from the oven and leave to cool.
13. Serve and enjoy!

Potato and leek soup

Servings: 4
Preparation time: 25 minutes

Ingredients:

2 potatoes, peeled and diced
600 ml vegetable stock
1 bay leaf
½ tsp oregano
1 leek, chopped
1 tbsp olive oil
120 ml coconut milk
2 thyme sprigs
3 garlic cloves, crushed
1 pinch of salt

Preparation:

1. Put the olive oil and leek in the pressure cooker and sauté briefly.
2. Add the salt and garlic. Sauté for one minute.
3. Add the potatoes, vegetable stock, bay leaf, oregano and thyme. Stir through.
4. Close the lid and cook at high pressure for 8 minutes.
5. Open with the cold water method.
6. Remove the bay leaf and puree the remaining contents.
7. Add coconut milk and mix well.
8. Serve warm.

Curry with spinach and potatoes

Servings: 6

Preparation time: 30 minutes

Ingredients:

1 kg baby spinach, chopped
1 onion, diced
2 tbsp olive oil
1 pinch cayenne pepper
1 tsp turmeric
1 tsp coriander
1 tsp cumin
1 potato, diced
750 ml vegetable stock without additives
3 cloves garlic, crushed
1 pinch of salt

Preparation:

1. Sauté olive oil and onions in saucepan for 5 minutes.
2. Add the garlic and stir well for 30 seconds.
3. Add the cayenne pepper, turmeric, coriander and cumin. Mix well.
4. Add the potatoes, vegetable stock, lentils and salt. Mix well.
5. Close the lid and cook at high pressure for 10 minutes.
6. Open with the cold water method.
7. Add the spinach. Mix well.
8. Serve hot. Rice is ideal as a side dish.

Rice chowder

Servings: 4
Preparation time: 70 minutes

Ingredients:

40 g raw cashews, soaked overnight and then drained.
½ medium potato, boiled with skin
120 g white beans
1 teaspoon extra virgin olive oil
½ yellow onion, diced
2 cloves garlic, crushed
½ bunch celery, diced
60 g whole grain rice, uncooked
60 g additional whole grain rice, soaked overnight and then drained
500 ml vegetable stock (alternatively: water)
1 tablespoon vinegar
Salt and pepper to taste
A pinch of parsley

Preparation:

1. Blend cashews, cooked potatoes and white beans in a blender. Add a little vegetable stock or water if necessary.
2. Heat the oil in a pot over medium heat. Add onions, garlic, celery and salt. Sauté for 3-5 minutes, stirring constantly.
3. Add both rice. Mix well and sauté for 1-2 minutes.
4. Add the vegetable stock and bring to the boil. Once boiling, reduce the heat to medium.
5. Add vinegar and a pinch of pepper to the pan.
6. Stir in cashew mixture and continue to simmer the soup, stirring constantly so that the rice does not stick to the bottom. Add more vegetable stock if needed to thin the soup.
7. Simmer for 30-45 minutes, respectively until the rice is heated through.
8. Season with salt and spices. Sprinkle with parsley. Done.

Coconut rice with turmeric

Servings: 8
Preparation time: 50 minutes

Ingredients:

900 g whole grain rice
840 ml coconut milk
1 pinch turmeric
1 pinch of cinnamon
1 pinch of clove powder or crushed cloves respectively
1 pinch of cardamom powder

Preparation:

1. Place the ingredients in the rice cooker and mix well.
2. Cook in the rice cooker on standard settings. Alternatively, cook in the saucepan for around 15-20 minutes.
3. When cooked, stir well again.
4. Serve while still warm.

Fennel ice tea

Servings: 10
Preparation time: 45 minutes

Ingredients:

170 g fennel seeds
1 tablespoon extra fennel seeds
2.5 litres of water
A few ice cubes

Preparation:

1. Bring the water to the boil.
2. Add the fennel seeds and continue to boil for about 30 minutes.
3. Leave to cool and then lower the temperature and leave to rest overnight in the fridge.
4. Serve the next day garnished with the additional fennel seeds and a few ice cubes.

Broccoli-Cauliflower Soup with Almond Milk

Servings: 2
Preparation time: 50 minutes

Ingredients:

500 g cauliflower, in florets
1 potato, peeled and diced
200 g broccoli
1 litre vegetable stock without additives
¼ tsp thyme
1 pinch of pepper
1 tsp garlic powder
3/2 tsp vinegar
2 tbsp lemon juice
120 ml almond milk, unsweetened
1 onion, diced
2 celery stalks
50 g carrots, sliced
1 pinch salt/pepper

Preparation:

1. Place potatoes, carrots, celery and cauliflower in pressure cooker.
2. Add vegetable stock and close lid. Cook for 4 minutes at high pressure.
3. Release the pressure normally.
4. Puree contents in saucepan.
5. Add the remaining ingredients and mix well.
6. Sauté again for 5 minutes until the broccoli is cooked through.
7. Enjoy.

Celery soup

Servings: 4
Preparation time: 40 minutes

Ingredients:

500 g celery, chopped
½ tsp dill
500 ml vegetable stock
250 ml coconut milk
1 onion, diced
1 pinch of salt

Preparation:

1. Place ingredients in pressure cooker.
2. Close lid and cook for 25 minutes. If using a food processor: select soup function and cook.
3. Open with the cold water method.
4. Puree until it forms a uniform mass.
5. Serve warm.

Steamed vegetables with mushrooms

Servings: 4
Preparation time: 30 minutes

Ingredients:

750 g potatoes, peeled and diced
2 carrots, peeled and chopped
1 celery bulb, chopped
1 leek, chopped
1 tbsp olive oil
1 mushroom, sliced
½ tsp herbs de Provence
500 ml vegetable stock
75 g peas
1 pinch of salt
1 pinch of pepper

Preparation:

1. Sauté olive oil and mushrooms for two minutes in a pressure cooker.
2. Add the celery, potatoes, carrots, herbs, vegetable stock, pepper and salt. Mix everything well.
3. Close the lid and cook gently at low pressure for 10 minutes.
4. Release the pressure normally and open the lid.
5. Add the peas. Stir well and sauté for one minute.
6. Serve warm.

Sweet potato wedges

Servings: 4-6
Preparation time: 25 minutes

Ingredients:

6 sweet potatoes, peeled and cut into wedges
4 tbsp coconut oil
1 tsp curry powder
1 pinch of salt
2 courgettes, spiralised or sliced very thinly

Preparation:

1. Preheat the oven to 220 degrees.
2. Mix the potatoes and coconut oil together with the salt and curry.
3. Spread the potatoes evenly on a baking tray. Leave to bake, turning occasionally.
4. After 15 minutes, sprinkle the courgettes over the baking tray and potatoes.
5. Bake for a further 5 minutes. Leave to cool briefly and enjoy

Spinach and chickpea salad

Servings: 2-4
Preparation time: 20 minutes

Ingredients:

200 g chickpeas, cooked
200 g spinach
1 avocado, diced
A few coriander leaves
1 onion, diced
2 courgettes, spiralised or thinly sliced
Juice of one lemon
2 tbsp coconut oil
1 pinch of salt
1 pinch black pepper
2 tbsp curry powder
Handful of sultanas
2 tbsp chia seeds

Preparation:

1. Heat the oil in a saucepan.
2. Add the courgette pieces one by one with the curry powder and salt and sauté. Add chickpeas and simmer for a few minutes, stirring constantly.
3. Remove from the heat and leave to cool. Meanwhile, combine avocado, sultanas, onion and baby spinach in a bowl. Add the courgette and chickpea mixture.
4. Add the remaining ingredients and sprinkle with lemon juice. Serve and enjoy.

Grilled halibut fillets

Portions: 2
Preparation time: 180 minutes

Ingredients:

2 halibut fillets, approx. 200 g
1 tbsp lemons
6 tbsp extra virgin olive oil
1 clove of garlic, crushed
1 tsp basil
1 tbsp parsley
1 tsp salt
1 tsp black pepper
Vegetable garnish of choice

Preparation:

1. Whisk together the garlic, basil, lemon juice, parsley, salt and pepper with the olive oil.
2. Pour the marinade over the halibut fillets and rub in gently. Refrigerate for 2 - 3 hours.
3. Preheat the grill to high heat and position the grates about 10 cm from the heat source.
4. Drain the excess marinade from the fillet and grill for about 5 minutes on each side, or until the fish is well cooked.
5. Serve warm with your favourite vegetables on the side.

Tofu and asparagus magic

Servings: 4
Preparation time: 30 minutes

Ingredients:

180 g tofu, cut into cubes
½ bunch asparagus, peeled
1 tsp stevia
A little vinegar
1 tsp sesame oil
1 tsp vegetable oil
1 clove of garlic, crushed
½ carrot, finely chopped

Preparation:

1. Mix all the ingredients together well in a large bowl.
2. Put the mixture into the rice cooker.
3. Sauté for 25 minutes. Add more vinegar and oil if necessary.
4. Stir through and serve.
5. Alternatively, sauté for 30 minutes in the steamer basket of the pressure cooker at low pressure.

Tofu with stuffed sweet potatoes from the oven

Servings: 3
Preparation time: 120 minutes

Ingredients:

1 large sweet potato
1/4 tablespoon olive oil
1/4 small onion, diced
1 clove garlic, crushed
1/2 teaspoon finely chopped rosemary
A pinch of red pepper flakes
Salt and pepper to taste
70 g kale, finely chopped
420 g firm tofu, cut into cubes
2 tablespoons water

Preparation:

1. Preheat the oven to 190°C. Line a baking tray with baking paper. Bake the sweet potato for one hour. Leave oven on.
2. Allow the potato to cool briefly. Cut open and scrape out the "flesh" and roughly chop. Set aside. Set the seeded potato aside as well.
3. Heat the oil in a large non-stick frying pan. Sauté the onions, garlic, rosemary, red pepper flakes in it for 3 minutes. Add cabbage and fry for five minutes, stirring occasionally. Stir in the "sweet potato meat" together with the tofu and water. Simmer for another minute.
4. Place the sweet potato skin or respectively the "cored" potato on the baking tray. Fill with the filling from the pan and bake covered with foil for 30 minutes.

Prawns with quinoa

Servings: 3
Preparation time: 25 minutes

Ingredients:

A little olive oil
170 g quinoa
500 ml chicken stock without additives
3 tablespoons coconut flakes
25 g grated carrots
40 g diced onions
1 tsp ginger, grated
½ tsp garlic, chopped
10 deveined prawns
lime juice
Coriander to garnish

Preparation:

1. Cook quinoa in vegetable broth according to package instructions.
2. Toast the coconut flakes in a medium frying pan. Set aside.
3. Drizzle olive oil over pan and sauté carrots and onions until soft.
4. Add the ginger and garlic and sauté for another minute. Then set aside.
5. Fry prawns (in the same) pan until golden brown. Once quinoa is cooked, add coconut flakes, onions, carrots, ginger and garlic.
6. Add the coriander and lime juice. Mix well.
7. Serve and garnish with prawns on top.

Courgette and prawn mix

Servings: 3

Preparation time: 70 minutes

Ingredients:

2 medium courgettes
12-15 large prawns, peeled, deveined
½ tbsp extra virgin olive oil
3 cloves garlic, crushed
1 tbsp parsley, chopped
2 tbsp lemon juice
Zest of ½ lemon
1 tbsp coconut oil
350 g baby spinach
A little salt
A little pepper

Preparation:

1. Devein and peel the prawns.
2. Crush the garlic.
3. Mix olive oil, 1 tablespoon lemon juice, garlic, parsley, peel, salt and pepper. Marinate for 30 minutes.
4. Make the pasta from the courgettes.
5. Put the pasta in a sieve and sprinkle with salt. Mix well and leave for 20 minutes.
6. Drain the courgettes and pat dry with kitchen towels.
7. Heat the coconut oil over a medium heat.
8. Add the prawns and marinade. Cook for 30 seconds.
9. Turn the prawns over and cook for another 30 seconds.
10. Set the prawns aside and then add the courgettes to the pan. Cook for one minute.
11. Add the spinach and parsley with the prawns.
12. Stir until the prawns are pink and the pasta is soft. (1-2 minutes)
13. Add the salt and pepper and another tablespoon of lemon juice. Garnish with the lemon zest.

Vegetable soup with beans and pumpkin

Servings: 3
Preparation time: 35 minutes
Do not prepare dish until the 3-4th week of the diet!

Ingredients:

1 tablespoon olive oil
1 medium onion, chopped
1 stalk of celery, sliced
1 medium carrot, chopped
1 teaspoon garlic, chopped
1400 ml chicken stock, without additives
250 g peeled butternut squash/musk squash
450 g dried tomatoes
600 g white beans - drained, rinsed
1 small courgette - halved lengthwise, sliced
175 g broccoli - cut into small florets
1 tablespoon fresh oregano
¼ teaspoon salt
¼ teaspoon pepper
A handful of parmesan cheese, grated

Preparation:

1. Heat the oil over medium heat in a slow cooker. Add the onion, carrots, celery and garlic and cook for 5 minutes.
2. Stir in the stock, tomatoes and pumpkin. Bring to a boil. Reduce the heat.
3. Cover and simmer for about 20 minutes. Add beans, broccoli, courgette, oregano, pepper and salt. Cook for 5 minutes. Sprinkle with grated Parmesan cheese before serving.

Corn and bean sprout salad

Servings: 4
Preparation time: 2 hours 15 minutes
Do not prepare dish until 3-4 weeks of diet!

Ingredients:

Corn on two cobs
200 g black bean sprouts, rinsed and drained
1 tomato, diced
½ pepper, finely chopped
¼ teaspoon chilli powder
¼ teaspoon sea salt
1 tablespoon lime juice
½ jalapeño, finely chopped
1 avocado, peeled and sliced
4 lime wedges, for garnish
1 tablespoon vinegar

Preparation:

1. Place beans in a bowl filled with water. Leave to soak for at least 12 hours - changing the water every 3 hours in between. Rinse and drain.
2. Put the corn kernels and beans in a bowl with the rest of the ingredients, except the avocado and lime wedges.
3. Mix well and cover with cling film and leave in the fridge for 2 hours to allow the flavour to develop.
4. Serve garnished with the avocado pieces and lime wedges.

Kukicha smoothie

Servings: 2

Preparation time: 5 minutes

Do not prepare dish until the 3-4th week of the diet!

Ingredients:

250 ml kukicha tea (green tea)
250 ml coconut milk
150 g spinach
1 banana
1 tsp ginger
1 apple (Granny Smith)
50 g almonds, soaked

Preparation:

1. Mix the ingredients in a blender.
2. Stir and serve.

Mashed potato with soy milk

Servings: 4
Preparation time: 20 minutes

Ingredients:

4 potatoes, floury, diced
4 tbsp parsley, chopped
150 ml soy milk
5 cloves garlic, crushed
250 ml vegetable stock
1 pinch of salt

Preparation:

1. Put the garlic, potatoes and vegetable stock in the pressure cooker.
2. Close the lid and cook at high pressure for 4 minutes.
3. Open with the cold water method.
4. Place the potatoes in a bowl. Add the soy milk.
5. Mash and make into a pulp.
6. Add parsley and salt. Mix well.
7. Serve warm.

Steamed potato salad

Servings: 4
Preparation time: 20 minutes
Do not prepare dish until 3-4 weeks of diet!

Ingredients:

250 ml water
750 g potatoes, floury and sliced
2 tbsp olive oil
2 tbsp rice wine vinegar
4 tbsp parsley, chopped
1 pinch of salt

Preparation:

1. Place steamer insert in pressure cooker. Fill with water.
2. Place potatoes in steamer insert and cook at high pressure for five minutes.
3. Open with the cold water method.
4. In a bowl, mix the onions, vinegar, pepper and salt.
5. Add the steamed potatoes and parsley. Mix well.
6. Serve the salad warm.
7. Optional: if you want it "chunkier", use waxy potatoes.

Chickpea curry with potatoes

Servings: 4
Preparation time: 15 minutes
Do not prepare dish until the 3-4th week of the diet!

Ingredients:

2 potatoes, peeled and diced
150 g chickpeas, cooked
½ tbsp cumin
1 onion, diced
1 tbsp extra virgin olive oil
¼ tsp ginger
1 tsp coriander
1 tsp turmeric
200 g tomatoes, chopped
1 pinch of salt

Preparation:

1. Put the oil, cumin and onion in the pressure cooker and sauté for 3 minutes.
2. Add the ginger, coriander, turmeric, tomatoes, salt and potatoes. Sauté for 2 minutes.
3. Add water to the saucepan.
4. Close the lid and cook at high pressure for 5 minutes.
5. Open with the cold water method.
6. Serve.

Chia Cinnamon Breakfast

Servings: 4
Preparation time: 20 minutes
Do not prepare dish until 3-4 weeks of diet!

Ingredients:

500 ml almond milk
500 ml water
2 tsp vanilla extract
200 g oat flakes
2 tbsp chia seeds
2 tsp cinnamon
1 tbsp gesture powder
Juice of one lemon
2 tbsp coconut oil
2 apples, peeled and diced (variety: Granny Smith)

Preparation:

1. Put oats in bowl with heated water. Mix and cover.
2. In the meantime, heat coconut oil in a frying pan over medium heat. Sauté apples in it.
3. Add sautéed apples to bowl. Add almond milk, chia seeds, vanilla extract and barley powder.
4. Sprinkle with lemon juice. Enjoy.

Pumpkin smoothie with olives and courgettes

Servings: 8
Preparation time: 25 minutes

Ingredients:

600 g pumpkin
600 g courgette (diced)
360 g fresh green olives
10 tbsp olive oil
400 g celery
2 tsp Himalayan salt/crystal salt
4 tbsp lemon juice
120 g coconut flesh (grated coconut if necessary)
500 ml coconut water
4 tbsp sesame seeds
A few ice cubes

Preparation:

1. Cut the pumpkin and courgette into small pieces and put them in a bowl with salt and lemon juice.
2. In the meantime, chop the olives (and pit them if necessary).
3. Blend the olives, pumpkin, courgette, celery and coconut water in a blender until smooth.
4. Add the olive oil and coconut meat. Blend again.
5. Toast the sesame seeds in a pan. Add a tablespoon of oil if necessary.
6. Pour the contents of the blender into a glass with the ice cubes.
7. Garnish with sesame seeds and serve.

Homemade spread with cashews

Servings: 4
Preparation time: 10 minutes

Ingredients:

150 g cashews
70 g pine nuts
1-3 tbsp stevia
1 teaspoon lemon juice
125 g walnuts, chopped or crushed
Slices of bread (wholemeal)

Preparation:

1. Process all ingredients except walnuts in a blender until uniform. Preparation time approx. 2-4 minutes.
2. Stir in walnuts and serve as a spread.
3. Keeps well packed in the fridge for 3-4 days.

Paleo Porridge with Walnut

Servings: 1
Preparation time: 10 minutes
Do not prepare dish until the 3-4th week of the diet!

Ingredients:

30 g walnut kernels
2 tbsp pumpkin seeds
1 tbsp chia seeds
1 tsp cinnamon
1 tsp nutmeg
250 ml coconut milk
1 tsp coconut oil
Juice of one lemon
Juice of one grapefruit

Preparation:

1. Mix ingredients in bowl and add coconut milk.
2. Stir and serve.

Slow Cooker Soup with Zucchini

Servings: 5
Preparation time: 7 hours
Prepare dish only from the 3-4th diet week!

Ingredients:

660 ml beef stock
1 medium courgette - Cut into spirals
2 stalks celery - Chopped
1 small onion - Diced
1 medium carrot - Chopped
1 medium tomato - Diced
1 ½ tsp garlic salt
750 g minced beef
100 g Parmesan cheese - Grated
6 cloves garlic - minced
1 large egg
4 tbsp parsley - chopped
1 ½ tsp sea salt
1 ½ tsp onion powder
1 tsp Italian herbs
1 tsp dried oregano
½ tsp pepper

Preparation:

1. Set the slow cooker to low heat.
2. Put in the beef stock, courgette, onion, celery, carrot, tomato and garlic salt. Cover the pot.
3. In a large bowl, combine the Parmesan, ground beef, egg, garlic, sea salt, parsley, onion powder, Italian herbs, pepper, and oregano. Mix well and form 30 patties.
4. Heat the oil over medium heat in a large frying pan. When the pan is hot, add the patties and fry until they are brown on all sides.
5. Place the meatballs in the slow cooker, close the lid and cook for 6 hours.

Slow Cooker Chili

Servings: 5
Preparation time: 8 hours
Do not prepare dish until 3-4 weeks of diet!

Ingredients:

1 kg beef
150 g onions - diced
400 g tomatoes - chopped
180 g peppers - diced
60 g serrano chilli - diced
1 ancho chilli/poblano - diced (alternative: hot chilli)
3 pasilla peppers - diced (or use hot chilli of choice)
250 ml beef stock - low sodium
200 ml water

Preparation:

1. Prepare the vegetables.
2. Place the meat in the cooker; layer the vegetables on top.
3. Cook on low for 6-8 hours.
4. Add the water.
5. Shred the meat with 2 forks and stir it back into the vegetables.

Coconut aubergines from the oven

Servings: 4

Preparation time: 1 hour 15 minutes

Ingredients:

1 aubergine, sliced
1 onion, diced
1 tsp chilli powder
500 ml coconut milk
1 pinch of salt
1 pinch of pepper

Preparation:

1. Preheat oven to 180 degrees. Lay out a layer of aubergine pieces in casserole dish. Place a layer of onions and spices on top.
2. Place another layer of aubergine pieces on top and cover again with onions and spices. Repeat until everything has been used up.
3. Lastly, pour the coconut milk over the top. Cover the casserole with aluminium foil and bake in the oven for 60 minutes.
4. Remove the foil and bake for another 10 minutes. Serve hot and enjoy.

Avocado and pumpkin salad

Servings: 4
Preparation time: 25 minutes

Ingredients:

500 g pumpkin, diced
1 tbsp olive oil
2 avocados, diced
Juice of one lemon
½ head lettuce

Dressing:

150 ml yoghurt
3 tbsp peppermint, chopped
1 tbsp stevia
2 tsp cumin
1 pinch salt
1 pinch black pepper

Preparation:

1. Preheat oven to 200 degrees. Spread pumpkin pieces evenly on baking tray and drizzle with olive oil.
2. Bake for 15 minutes. Leave the baked pumpkin pieces to cool. Mix all dressing ingredients.
3. Arrange lettuce leaves on plates and place squash pieces on top. Pour dressing over top.
4. Enjoy.

Slow Cooker Pasta with Tomatoes

Servings: 3
Preparation time: 4 hours 10 minutes
Do not prepare dish until 3-4 weeks of diet!

Ingredients:

10 plum tomatoes, chopped
½ onion, diced
1 tsp garlic powder
60 ml olive oil
1 tsp oregano
1 tsp basil
1 tsp cayenne pepper
1 tsp salt
1 tsp pepper
1 pinch cinnamon
150 g wholegrain Farfalle noodles

Preparation:

1. Chop everything as necessary.
2. Put the ingredients in a slow cooker.
3. Cook on high for four hours.
4. Serve and enjoy.
5. Optional: 20 minutes before the end of cooking, add a little chilli powder and mix for a spicy flavour.

Chicken noodle mix in the slow cooker

Servings: 5
Preparation time: 20 minutes

Ingredients:

180 g wholegrain spaghetti
480 g frozen vegetable mix
3 tablespoons peanut butter
1 tablespoon stevia
2 tablespoons soy sauce - low sodium
2 tablespoons water
1 tablespoon vegetable oil
2 cloves garlic - chopped
¼ teaspoon red pepper - crushed
250 g chicken - fried
40 g peanuts - chopped

Preparation:

1. Cook the spaghetti in a slow cooker according to the packet instructions. Add the vegetables in the last few minutes and then drain.
2. In a small pan, mix the sugar, peanut butter, soy sauce, oil, water, garlic and crushed pepper. Heat everything until melted. Stir frequently.
3. In a large mixing bowl, combine the noodles, shredded chicken and peanut sauce.

Cheese macaroni in the slow-cooker

Servings: 6
Preparation time: 5 hours

Ingredients:

2 eggs
400 ml milk
360 g condensed milk
250 g wholegrain macaroni
400 g grated cheddar
1 tsp salt
½ tsp pepper

Preparation:

1. Put everything in the slow cooker and stir well.
2. Cook on low for 5 hours, stirring occasionally.
3. serve and enjoy

Pressure cooker noodles with cheese

Servings: 4
Preparation time: 20 minutes

Ingredients:

300 g pasta, gluten-free, wholegrain
60 g butter
200 g cheddar cheese, grated
1 cup whipped cream
250 ml vegetable stock
1 pinch of pepper
1 pinch of salt

Preparation:

1. Put the whipped cream, noodles and vegetable stock in a pressure cooker.
2. Close the lid and cook for 7 minutes.
3. Open the lid with the cold water method.
4. Add butter and cheese. Stir until melted.
5. Season with pepper and salt.
6. Serve and enjoy.

Oven soup with onions

Servings: 4
Preparation time: 2 hours 40 minutes

Ingredients:

5 large onions
2 tbsp olive oil
1 tbsp butter
60 ml vermouth
2 litres vegetable stock
Salt and pepper to taste
A little thyme to garnish

Preparation:

1. Preheat the oven to 200°C. Slice the onions very thinly. Pour olive oil into a fire pot (or ceramic pot). Line with the onions. Cover and put in the oven.
2. Bake for 90 minutes - stirring briefly inside every 20 minutes. Remove the fire pot from the oven. Put the lid down and add the butter (and optional vermouth). Mix well until butter is completely liquefied. Add vegetable stock and cover again. Bake in the oven for another hour.
3. Season to taste with salt and pepper. Serve garnished with thyme and enjoy.

Courgette chips

Servings: 4
Preparation time: 55 minutes

Ingredients:

2 courgettes, cut into thick slices
25 g breadcrumbs from wholegrain bread
25 g parmesan
2 tsp cooking oil
1 tbsp extra virgin olive oil
1 pinch of salt
A little ground black pepper

Preparation:

1. Preheat the oven to 230°C.
2. Spray the baking tray with cooking spray (or grease with the oil) and set aside.
3. In a mixing bowl, mix the sliced courgette pieces with the oil.
4. In another bowl, mix the courgette pieces with the oil.
5. In another bowl, mix the Parmesan with the salt, pepper and breadcrumbs.
6. Add the courgettes to the Parmesan mixture and mix well.
7. Place the courgette slices on the baking tray and bake for about 30 minutes, or until the courgettes are brown and crisp.
8. Serve hot!

Salad with halloumi

Servings: 2
Preparation time: 55 minutes
Do not prepare dish until the 3-4th week of diet!

Ingredients:

Salad:

2 aubergines
1 large pepper
3 roma tomatoes
½ large onion
5 garlic cloves
2 tbsp olive oil
230 g halloumi cheese
120 g spinach

Pesto dressing:

40 g coarsely chopped parsley
60 g walnuts
2 tbsp olive oil
2 tbsp water
Juice of a quarter of a lemon
¼ tsp salt to taste

Preparation:

1. Preheat the oven to 200°C. Line a baking tray with baking paper. Clean the aubergines and cut into rings (about 1 cm thick). Halve and clean the peppers, respectively remove the seeds and the whites. Halve and seed the tomatoes. Roughly dice the onion. Place all the vegetables and garlic cloves on the baking tray. Bake for about 40 minutes, drizzled with olive oil.
2. In the meantime, cut the halloumi into approx. 15 cm slices. When the 40 minutes are up, make a little space for the cheese and place it on the baking tray. Bake for another five minutes with the cheese. Use the oven's grill function (or simply turn up the heat on the convection oven slightly) to bake the cheese for 3-5 minutes until golden brown. Be careful not to burn the cheese!
3. In the meantime, mix the pesto ingredients in a blender until a uniform mixture has formed. If necessary, add a little water or olive oil to achieve a more liquid consistency. Season to taste with salt.
4. Remove from the oven and thinly slice the tomatoes and peppers. Put the pesto and baked ingredients in a bowl. Mix with the spinach and serve.

Aubergine soup with tomatoes

Servings: 2
Preparation time: 1 hour 30 minutes
Do not prepare dish until 3-4 weeks of diet!

Ingredients:

2 large tomatoes
1 large aubergine
1 large red or yellow pepper
5 garlic cloves
1 tbsp olive oil
500 ml vegetable stock
120 ml cooking cream
2 tsp smoked paprika powder
½ tsp salt
½ tsp garlic powder
½ tsp cayenne pepper
Wholemeal croutons
Coriander or parsley to garnish

Preparation:

1. Preheat the oven to 200°C. Cut the vegetables in half lengthwise. Remove the green from the tomatoes and aubergine. Remove the inside of the peppers.
2. Place the vegetables on a baking tray lined with baking paper - open side up. Spread the garlic cloves evenly on the tray and drizzle the vegetables with olive oil.
3. Bake in the oven for 1 hour and 20 minutes. Halfway through, turn the vegetables once. If the garlic is in danger of burning, simply "cover" with the pepper halves.
4. Optionally, peel the skin off the vegetables.
5. Coarsely chop the finished vegetables and blend with the vegetable stock in a blender.
6. Add the rest of the ingredients to the soup and heat slightly if necessary. Serve and enjoy.

Paleo Sweet Potato Pasta

Servings: 1
Preparation time: 45 minutes

Ingredients:

1 large (inside) white sweet potato - Peeled, cut into spirals
3 tbsp coconut oil - melted
½ tsp sea salt
½ tsp pepper

Preparation:

1. Preheat the oven to 190°C.
2. Stir to coat the sweet potato with the coconut oil and spices.
3. Bake in the oven for 35 minutes.

Sweet potatoes with chickpeas and coconut

Servings: 3
Preparation time: 2 hours

Ingredients:

3 sweet potatoes
120 ml coconut milk
70 g almond butter
1 tbsp soy sauce
1 tbsp chilli sauce
1 tsp olive oil
1 tsp paprika powder
2 cloves garlic, crushed
2 drops stevia
1 pinch salt
2 tbsp coconut oil
200 g chickpeas, cooked and drained
1 red pepper, chopped
1 pinch garlic powder
1 pinch of pepper
2 onions, diced
1 tbsp coriander
A handful of cashew nuts

Preparation:

1. Preheat oven to 200°C.
2. Cut the potatoes in half with a knife.
3. Bake in the oven for 80 minutes wrapped in foil.
4. Blend garlic, paprika, olive oil, garlic sauce, soy sauce, coconut milk and almond butter in a blender. Sweeten with stevia.
5. Sauté the red pepper, onion and chickpeas in coconut oil for five minutes.
6. Smear jacket potato halves with sautéed ingredients and the blended paste.
7. Garnish with coriander and cashews.
8. Enjoy.

Roasted Brussels sprouts

Servings: 2
Preparation time: 1 hour

Ingredients:

750 g Brussels sprouts, chopped
3 tablespoons olive oil
1 teaspoon salt
½ teaspoon black pepper

Preparation:

1. Preheat oven to 200°C.
2. Place Brussels sprouts in bowl. Season with olive oil, salt and pepper.
3. Spread on a baking tray. Place in the oven on the middle shelf.
4. Roast in the oven for 30-45 minutes. Occasionally take out the baking tray and shake a little so that nothing burns and everything is browned evenly.
5. Enjoy hot.

Artichoke dip with peppers

Servings: 5
Preparation time: 40 minutes
Do not prepare dish until 3-4 weeks of diet!

Ingredients:

2 tsp. chopped red peppers
2 tsp chopped spring onions
45 g crumbled wholegrain bread as breadcrumb substitute
240 g almond butter
230 g light mayonnaise
1 clove garlic, pressed
1 tsp cayenne pepper
60 g chopped red pepper
50 g chopped spring onions
450 g chopped artichoke hearts
600 g cooked crab meat

Preparation:

1. Preheat the oven to 180°C.
2. Put the mayonnaise and cream cheese in a mixing bowl and mix until smooth.
3. Add the garlic and artichoke hearts, the crabmeat, the parmesan cheese, the spring onions, the red peppers and the cayenne pepper.
4. Put the mixture in a baking dish and sprinkle with the breadcrumbs.
5. Place in the oven and bake for 30 minutes.
6. Remove from the oven and leave to cool for a few minutes.
7. Serve and enjoy!

Apple dip with coconut oil and rice milk

Servings: 4
Preparation time: 20 minutes
Do not prepare dish until 3-4 weeks of diet!

Ingredients:

10 large carrots, sliced
8 apples, peeled, cored and sliced
100 g agar as a substitute for gelatine
4 tablespoons cinnamon
1 tablespoon sesame powder
2 tablespoons coconut oil
500 ml rice milk
1500 ml water

Preparation:

1. Bring water to the boil. Add the carrots, cinnamon, apples and agar. 2.
2. Turn off the heat when it boils. Add the rice milk and stir well. Cover and leave to cool.
3. Finally, puree all the ingredients with a blender. Add the sesame powder and coconut oil for a better consistency and more flavour.
4. Serve this dip with organic rice cakes.

Chilli dressing

Servings: 6
Preparation time: 10 minutes
Do not prepare dish until 3-4 weeks of diet!

Ingredients:

2 chillies, fresh
120 ml extra virgin olive oil
3 tbsp lemon juice
1 tbsp lime juice
A handful of mint leaves, finely chopped
3 tbsp coconut milk
1 pinch of salt
1 pinch of pepper

Preparation:

1. Peel the chilli pepper. Remove the seeds.
2. Chop the chilli and mix with lemon/lime juice, coconut milk, mint and olive oil.
3. Add salt and pepper. Drizzle over the salad to be garnished.
4. Optional: also suitable as a fiery dip.

Guacamole dip

Servings: 6

Preparation time: 1 hour 10 minutes

Ingredients:

6 avocados, halved, pitted and peeled
Juice of two limes
1 teaspoon salt
1 teaspoon ground cumin
1 teaspoon cayenne pepper
1 onion, diced
1 tablespoon fresh coriander
1 clove garlic, crushed

Preparation:

1. In a mixing bowl, combine the lime juice and the avocado flesh. Then mash the whole thing with a potato masher. Season with salt, cumin and cayenne pepper. Mix well again.
2. Fold in the onions, coriander and garlic. Cover the bowl with foil and leave at room temperature for an hour to allow the flavours to develop.
3. Eat on the same day or chilled in the fridge the next day at the latest.

Hummus with chickpeas

Servings: 11
Preparation time: 10 minutes
Do not prepare dish until the 3-4th week of the diet!

Ingredients:

200 g chickpeas, cooked, drained.
50 g red pepper, chopped, roasted
3 garlic cloves, crushed
½ jalapeno, crushed
1 pinch of salt
1 pinch of pepper
4 tbsp olive oil
2 tbsp coriander
Juice of one lemon
A little water

Preparation:

1. Blend the chickpeas, coriander, pepper, garlic and jalapeno in a blender.
2. Add the olive oil, lemon juice and water (if using) and blend until the desired consistency is reached. Season and salt.
3. Serve. Optional: Ideal as a dip or with fresh vegetables.

Nori rolls

Servings: 4
Preparation time: 25 minutes

Ingredients:

"Sushi" filling:

140 g almonds
300 g cashew nuts
1 tablespoon fresh ginger, ground
1 clove garlic, chopped
3 carrots, chopped
40 g onions, diced
75 g sultanas (for the first two weeks: dried)
1 teaspoon sea salt
2 tablespoons extra virgin olive oil

Wraps:

4 nori leaves
A handful of spinach leaves, well rinsed and then drained

Sauce:

Coconut aminos or soy sauce

Preparation:

1. **"Sushi"** :
2. Grind almonds and cashews to a fine powder.
3. Then combine the ginger, garlic, carrots, onions, sultanas and sea salt and blend in a blender. Add the olive oil, lemon juice and almond-cashew mixture. Blend everything together well.
4. **Nori wrap:** Lay out 3. Nori sheets on kitchen work surface. Place dried spinach leaves on the bottom half of each nori sheet. Put about ¼ of the "sushi mixture" on the spinach per sheet.
5. Roll up the nori leaves and cut into 6 rolls with a sharp knife.
6. Serve with coconut aminos or soy sauce as a dip.

Bean burger with carrots

Servings: 1
Preparation time: 25 minutes

Ingredients:

1 tablespoon diced onion
1 tablespoon carrot, grated
1 tablespoon bread crumbs
45 g kidney beans, rinsed and drained
45 g navy beans, rinsed and drained
½ tablespoon parsley, finely chopped
A pinch of chilli powder
Salt and pepper to taste
1 teaspoon carob bean gum (as a flour substitute)
3 tablespoons extra virgin olive oil (for frying)
One wholemeal hamburger bun

Preparation:

1. Put half of the bread crumbs in a mixing bowl.
2. Sauté 1 tablespoon of olive oil in a medium pot with the onions for 3 minutes. Add the carrots and sauté for another 2-3 minutes. Then add the mixture to the breadcrumbs.
3. In a bowl, roughly mash the beans with a fork. Then add to the carrot mixture. Season with salt, pepper and chilli powder.
4. In a bowl, mix the remaining breadcrumbs with the flour, parsley, salt and pepper.
5. Shape the bean-carrot mixture into 1-2 burger patties/"vegan patties". Then "bread" them thoroughly with the flour mixture.
6. Heat 2 tablespoons of olive oil in a frying pan over medium heat. Fry the burger patties for approx. 5 minutes on both sides until golden brown.
7. Place the patties on the burger buns. Add the desired seasoning and - if desired - e.g. pieces of tomato, lettuce leaves or similar to round off.

Quinoa-pumpkin porridge

Servings: 2

Preparation time: 15 minutes

Ingredients:

250 ml almond milk
250 ml water
170 g quinoa
115 g pumpkin, pureed
1 tsp cinnamon
2 tbsp linseed, ground
Juice of one lemon

Preparation:

1. Mix water and milk. Bring the mixture to the boil in a saucepan. Add remaining ingredients except flaxseed and lemon juice.
2. Simmer for 10 minutes until all the liquid has been absorbed. Remove from heat and add flaxseed meal.
3. Mix and pour into small serving bowls in batches.
4. Drizzle with lemon juice.
5. Optionally, top with pumpkin seeds as a garnish.

Slow Cooker Tomato and Pumpkin Goulash

Servings: 3
Preparation time: 4 hours
Do not prepare dish until 3-4 weeks of diet!

Ingredients:

6 tomatoes, diced
1 tbsp stevia
2 tbsp olive oil
1 onion, diced
1 tsp ginger powder
1 tsp cinnamon
1 tsp cumin
1 tbsp coriander
200 g chickpeas
1.5 kg pumpkin, peeled and cut into bite-sized pieces
1 tsp salt
1 tsp carob bean gum as a flour substitute
50 ml water

Preparation:

1. Chop the ingredients as necessary.
2. Put the ingredients into the slow cooker and mix.
3. Cook on a high heat for four hours.
4. Done.

Chicken breast with spinach and coconut

Servings: 2
Preparation time: 25 minutes

Ingredients:

1 chicken breast
600 g baby spinach
1 large onion - diced
120 ml coconut milk
3 tbsp coconut oil
1 handful of almonds
1 pinch of salt
1 pinch of pepper

Preparation:

1. Chop the almonds in a food processor and lightly toast them in a pan with the coconut oil. Set aside.
2. Place the coconut milk and spinach in a medium pot. Cover and simmer over a low heat.
3. Fry the onions in a frying pan for about 2 minutes.
4. Cut the chicken into squares.
5. Place in a pan and cook well for a few minutes.
6. Add the chicken and onions to the pot with the coconut milk and spinach. Stir and cover for 2 minutes.
7. Serve with the almonds on the side.

Date Camomile Tea

Servings: 4
Preparation time: 45 minutes

Ingredients:

50 g chamomile flowers
100 g parsley
1 litre water
4 tbsp dates
4 tablespoons mint

Preparation:

1. Bring water to the boil.
2. Using a ladle, pour a little water over the dates to soak.
3. Process the dates in a blender to a puree.
4. Wash the camomile and chop roughly.
5. Also wash the parsley thoroughly and chop coarsely.
6. Put the camomile and parsley in a bowl; pour boiling water over them.
7. Leave to stand for 20 minutes and then strain off the liquid.
8. Heat the liquid again briefly on the cooker.
9. Pour the liquid into a cup and stir in a little date puree.
10. Serve garnished with mint leaves.

Spinach and Cabbage Juice with Cucumber

Servings: 3

Preparation time: 20 minutes

Do not prepare dish until the 3-4th week of diet!

Ingredients:

450 g spinach

140 g cabbage

4 cucumbers

1 apple (Granny Smith)

1 litre coconut water

A few mint leaves

A few ice cubes

Preparation:

1. Wash the spinach and cabbage.
2. Put both in ice water.
3. Cut the cucumber and apple into small pieces.
4. Juice the above ingredients with a juicer.
5. Pour into a glass and stir in the coconut water.
6. Roughly chop the mint and stir in. Add a few ice cubes.
7. Serve cold.
8. Enjoy.

Apple-pumpkin curry with lentils

Servings: 3
Preparation time: 2 hours
Do not prepare dish until 3-4 weeks of diet!

Ingredients:

65 g red lentils & 65 g brown lentils
650 ml water
1/8 teaspoon turmeric
1 teaspoon extra virgin olive oil
1/4 onion, diced
3 tomatoes, diced
1 clove garlic, crushed
2 teaspoons curry powder
3/4 teaspoon ground cumin
1/8 teaspoon salt
1/8 teaspoon black pepper
1/8 teaspoon ground cloves
150 g pumpkin, without skin, cut into cubes
1/2 potato, diced
1 carrot, diced
1 apple (Granny Smith), cored and diced

Preparation:

1. Put lentils in a pot with water and turmeric. Cook on low to medium heat for about 45 minutes until nice and soft. Then drain. Keep 250 ml of the liquid (that is left over from the cooking).
2. Heat oil in a pot over medium heat. Stir in onion and sauté for 5 minutes until translucent. Add the tomatoes and garlic. Sauté for another 5 minutes, stirring occasionally.
3. Stir in the curry powder, cumin, salt, pepper and cloves. Add the 250 ml cooking liquid. Add the lentils, pumpkin, potatoes and carrots as well. Cook over a medium heat for 35-45 minutes until the vegetables have softened.
4. Stir in the apple pieces. Cook for another 15 minutes. Done.

Rice with prawns and coconut

Servings: 4
Preparation time: 25 minutes

Ingredients:

500 g king prawns; peeled and deveined
6 large garlic cloves; chopped
350 ml water
1 pinch of salt
1 jalapeno; stalked and seeded
1 lime
1 tablespoon olive oil
170 ml coconut milk
1 teaspoon red chilli powder
coriander
Wild rice (as a side dish, cooked according to package instructions)

Preparation:

1. Mince the garlic with water and ½ teaspoon salt in a blender. Make sure that semi-coarse pieces of garlic still remain.
2. Pour the mixture over the prawns and leave for 10 minutes.
3. Pour off the water from the prawns and garlic.
4. Now add the lime juice, ½ teaspoon of salt and the jalapeno.
5. Heat a tablespoon of olive oil over a high heat in a large frying pan.
6. Then add the prawns and cook for 1 minute.
7. Now add a small can of coconut milk and cook for another 30 seconds.
8. Stir in the chilli powder.
9. Pour the coconut mixture over the cooked rice.
10. Serve the dish. Enjoy your meal.

Rice with coconut and ginger

Servings: 2
Preparation time: 30 minutes
Do not prepare dish until the 3-4th week of diet!

Ingredients:

1 tablespoon vegetable oil
½ onion; small and finely chopped
1 clove of garlic; finely chopped
1 tablespoon ginger; grated
200 g wild rice, cooked
250 ml coconut milk
1 ½ tablespoons chicken stock
300 ml water
150 g sultanas

Preparation:

1. Heat the oil in a large frying pan over a medium heat.
2. Fry the onion, ginger, garlic and rice until the rice is brown.
3. Stir in the coconut milk and stock.
4. Bring everything to the boil over a high heat.
5. Reduce the heat to medium and cook for 5 minutes. Stir frequently.
6. Add the water and bring to the boil again.
7. Reduce the heat to low and simmer for 10 minutes.
8. Stir in the sultanas and bring to the boil over high heat.
9. Reduce the heat to low and simmer, covered, for another 5 minutes.

Entrecôte with coconut

Servings: 10
Preparation time: 3 hours

Ingredients:

1x 5 kg prime rib/entrecôte
10 garlic cloves; chopped
2 tablespoons coconut oil
2 teaspoons salt
2 teaspoons black pepper
2 teaspoons thyme

Preparation:

1. Place the prime ribs, fat side up, in a roasting pan.
2. Put the coconut oil, garlic, salt, thyme and pepper in a medium-sized mixing bowl.
3. Spread the mixture over the fat part of the prime rib and leave at room temperature for 45 minutes.
4. Preheat the oven to 260°C.
5. Bake the prime ribs for 20 minutes and then reduce the heat to 160°C.
6. Bake the prime ribs for a further 60 to 75 minutes.
7. Let the meat rest for 10 to 15 minutes before slicing.

Steak dry marinade

Servings: 4 meals
Preparation time: 10 minutes

Ingredients:

2 ½ teaspoons cinnamon - ground
2 teaspoons oregano
1 teaspoon chilli powder
1 teaspoon cumin
1 teaspoon salt
½ teaspoon pepper
½ teaspoon garlic powder
¼ teaspoon onion powder
¼ teaspoon cayenne pepper

Preparation:

1. Mix the ingredients together in a bowl.
2. Store in an airtight container.

Tropical curry mix

Servings: 4 meals
Preparation time: 10 minutes

Ingredients:

20 g whole coriander seeds
2 tablespoons whole cumin seeds
2 tablespoons whole anise seeds
1 tablespoon whole fenugreek seeds
1 tablespoon whole allspice berries
5 tablespoons turmeric

Preparation:

1. Combine ingredients in a bowl.
2. Blend in a blender.
3. Store in an airtight container.

Shrimps with jalapeno and chickpeas

Servings: 2

Preparation time: 20 minutes plus 2 hours chilling time

Do not prepare dish until 3-4 weeks of diet!

Ingredients:

1 tablespoon olive oil
1 jalapeno, diced, without seeds
1 clove garlic, crushed
3 tablespoons lime juice
100 g chickpeas
210 g shrimps (pre-cooked)
Chipotle/smoked jalapenos (2 tablespoons, in Mexican adobo sauce, chopped)
150 g red onion, diced
600 g tomatoes, diced
15 g coriander, chopped

Preparation:

1. Put chipotle, red onion, garlic, olive oil and jalapeno in a bowl; stir together until well mixed.
2. Add the lime juice, chickpeas, tomatoes and coriander to the mixture and mix.
3. Season to taste, then chill in the fridge for at least 2 hours.
4. Rinse the pre-cooked shrimps if necessary and serve with the chickpea mixture.

Hummus with tahina

Servings: 2

Preparation time: 12-24 hours respectively 40 min cooking time

Ingredients:

200 g chickpeas
1 tbsp tahina paste
3 tbsp olive oil
1 tsp cumin, ground
1 tsp coriander, ground
2 cloves garlic
60 ml lemon juice
1 pinch salt/pepper

Preparation:

1. Soak the chickpeas overnight in 1.5 litres of water.
2. Rinse the chickpeas and place in the rice cooker.
3. Cover with water so that the surface of the water overlaps the chickpeas by about 2 cm.
4. Cook on the white rice/standard setting.
5. Using a blender or food processor, blend together the finished chickpeas and remaining ingredients until uniform.
6. Finished.

Pumpkin Seed Coconut Smoothie

Servings: 3
Preparation time: 35 minutes

Ingredients:

4 tbsp flax seeds
4 tbsp sesame seeds
4 tbsp pumpkin seeds
4 tbsp sunflower seeds
10 tbsp almonds
50 g coconut cream
500 ml coconut water
300 g coconut meat
A pinch of (Himalayan) salt

Preparation:

1. Put the flax seeds, sesame seeds, pumpkin seeds and sunflower seeds in a pan and heat/roast for a few minutes on a low heat.
2. Blend the coconut meat and coconut water in a blender until smooth.
3. Remove the seeds from the pan and grind to a coarse powder.
4. Roughly chop the almonds and add to the kernels.
5. Add the kernels with the almonds to the coconut meat mixture.
6. Heat on a low heat (in a pan or pot) for five minutes so that the nutty flavour can develop.
7. Carefully spoon the coconut cream onto the finished smoothie - sprinkle with more almonds if necessary.
8. Serve and enjoy.

Mung beans with wild rice and turmeric

Servings: 6
Preparation time: 25 minutes

Ingredients:

500 g wild rice
2 tbsp coriander, chopped
1 tbsp olive oil
1 tsp turmeric
100 g mung beans
1 tbsp butter
500 ml vegetable stock
½ tsp salt

Preparation:

1. Rinse and dry the mung beans.
2. Put the butter and olive oil in a pressure cooker and sauté.
3. When oil is hot, add turmeric and stir for 30 seconds.
4. Add rice and mung beans and mix well.
5. Add salt and vegetable stock.
6. Close the lid and cook for 6 minutes at high pressure.
7. Release the pressure normally and open the lid.
8. Garnish with coriander.
9. Serve.

Seafood seasoning mix

Servings: 4 meals
Preparation time: 10 minutes

Ingredients:

6 1/3 tablespoons salt
3 2/3 tablespoons celery seeds
2 ½ teaspoons mustard powder (or ground mustard seeds)
2 ½ teaspoons red pepper flakes
1 ½ teaspoon pepper
1 ½ teaspoon bay leaves - ground
1 ½ teaspoon paprika
1 teaspoon ground cloves
1 teaspoon allspice
1 teaspoon ground ginger
¾ teaspoon cardamom
½ teaspoon cinnamon

Preparation:

1. Mix the ingredients in a bowl.
2. Store in an airtight container.

Steamed Cabbage Nut Pies

Servings: 3
Preparation time: 20 minutes

Ingredients:

170 g cauliflower, finely chopped
90 g broccoli, finely chopped
100 g butternut squash/musk squash, diced
35 g almonds, raw
100 g walnuts, raw
20 g sunflower seeds
¼ teaspoon cumin seeds
1/8 teaspoon ground black pepper
½ teaspoon salt
1 tablespoon vegetable oil, of your choice

Preparation:

1. Place steamer basket in a pot and fill with water accordingly.
2. Bring to the boil. Add pumpkin cubes and steam for 7-10 minutes.
3. Put the pumpkin pieces into a bowl and mash.
4. Now repeat the steaming process with broccoli and cauliflower. Approx. 2-6 minutes until the vegetables have softened.
5. Process walnuts, almonds, sunflower seeds in a food processor until uniform and a coarse breadcrumb-like consistency has been achieved. Now add the broccoli and cauliflower - continue blending.
6. Mix the pumpkin, salt, cumin and pepper with the blended mixture.
7. Divide into four equal portions. Shape into patties with your hands.
8. Heat the oil in a frying pan over medium heat. Fry the patties for 2 minutes on both sides so that they are nicely browned.

Quinoa with parsley

Servings: 4
Preparation time: 15 minutes

Ingredients:

340 g quinoa
2 tbsp parsley, finely chopped
Juice of one lemon
750 ml water
1 pinch of salt

Preparation:

1. Put the ingredients in a pressure cooker.
2. Close lid and boil at high pressure for 1 minute.
3. Let the pressure escape normally.
4. Serve warm.

Mushroom risotto with thyme

Servings: 4
Preparation time: 30 minutes
Do not prepare dish until 3-4 weeks of diet!

Ingredients:

450 g wild rice
2 tsp extra virgin olive oil
15 g butter
100 g Parmesan cheese, grated
1 litre vegetable stock
4 tbsp red wine
1 sprig of thyme
250 g mushrooms, halved (e.g. pickled mushrooms)
1 onion, diced
1 pinch of pepper
1 pinch of salt

Preparation:

1. Heat the olive oil in a quick-boiler.
2. When the oil is hot, add the onions and sauté them.
3. Add the mushrooms and thyme. Sauté as well.
4. Add the rice and stir-fry for 2 minutes.
5. Add the vegetable stock and red wine.
6. Add pepper and salt to taste.
7. Close lid and cook at high pressure for 7 minutes.
8. Open the lid with cold water method.
9. Add butter and cheese and stir until both are completely melted. Enjoy warm.

Paleo Almond Porridge

Servings: 3
Preparation time: 10 minutes

Ingredients:

100 g almonds, chopped
20 g coconut, chopped
2 tbsp pumpkin seeds
2 tbsp chia seeds
1 tbsp linseed
1 tsp cinnamon
1 tsp almond extract
500 ml water
Natural yoghurt to taste

Preparation:

1. Grind dry ingredients minus spices in blender.
2. Heat the water and then add the powder.
3. Mix well. Season and serve with yoghurt. Enjoy.

Pistou soup

Servings: 5
Preparation time: 45 minutes

Ingredients:

4 tbsp olive oil
1 leek, chopped
4 celery stalks, chopped
1 onion, diced
750 g frozen vegetable mix
1 can navy beans, washed and dried
1 pinch thyme
1 pinch of rosemary
2 bay leaves
1 litre water
1 pinch of salt
1 pinch of pepper

Pistou:

2 cloves of garlic, crushed
1 tomato, sliced (from the third week of the diet)
A few basil leaves
8 tbsp olive oil
1 pinch of salt

Preparation:

1. Heat oil in a pot and sauté leek, celery, onion and garlic. Add salt/pepper and add remaining ingredients (except pistou ingredients). Simmer for 5 minutes. Add the water and bring to the boil. Then simmer for 30 minutes.
2. Pistou: Crush the garlic and salt with a mortar. Add the tomatoes, basil leaves and olive oil and blend into a paste. Serve the finished soup and garnish with a little pistou paste. Enjoy.

Spicy turkey stew

Servings: 5
Preparation time: 5 hours

Ingredients:

240 g butternut/musk squash, peeled and diced
500 g turkey stew
1 large potato, peeled and diced
3 medium carrots, peeled and chopped
1 onion, diced
4 garlic cloves, crushed
1 tsp cumin
1 tsp chilli powder
150 g roasted chilli
1 litre chicken stock
1 pinch black pepper

Topping:

Juice of one lemon
2-3 tbsp coriander
1-2 tsp stevia

Preparation:

1. Fry the turkey in a pan.
2. Place the meat in the slow cooker with the remaining ingredients except the topping. Mix well.
3. Cook on high for 4-5 hours.
4. 4. 20 minutes before serving, stir in lemon juice and coriander. Add a little chicken stock if necessary.

Paleo Shepherd's Pie

Servings: 4
Preparation time: 1 hour

Ingredients:

500 g lamb or beef - chopped
1 medium courgette - chopped
1 yellow pumpkin - chopped
4 medium sweet potatoes - chopped
130 ml coconut milk
A little chilli powder
A little garlic powder
1 pinch of salt
1 pinch of pepper

Preparation:

1. Preheat your oven to 180°C.
2. Heat the coconut oil in a large frying pan over medium heat.
3. Add the minced meat and fry for 10 minutes.
4. Add the chopped courgette and yellow squash to the meat along with all the spices. Fry for another 10 minutes.
5. Bring a pot of water to the boil and add the sweet potatoes.
6. Boil for 20-25 minutes until cooked.
7. Drain and season with coconut milk, pepper and salt. If necessary, use a potato masher and mash to a pulp.
8. Place the meat and vegetables in an oven pan (23 x 33 cm).
9. Put the mashed potatoes on top.
10. Place in the oven and bake for 15 minutes.

Paleo sweet potatoes with salad

Servings: 3
Preparation time: 20 minutes

Ingredients:

3 sweet potatoes, diced
3 tablespoons extra virgin olive oil
2 cloves garlic, crushed
A pinch of sea salt
A pinch of black pepper
300 g kale, de-stemmed and cut into small pieces
1 tablespoon balsamic vinegar
1 tablespoon chives, finely chopped
½ teaspoon red pepper flakes

Preparation:

1. Light the grill and "preheat."
2. First grill the sweet potatoes for 3-5 minutes until they are nice and soft and browned.
3. Add the cabbage (on aluminium foil). Grill for 3-5 minutes.
4. Put the cabbage and potatoes in a bowl.
5. Add remaining ingredients and mix.
6. Enjoy cold or warm.

Spaghetti squash from the oven

Servings: 2

Preparation time: 1 hour 20 minutes

Ingredients:

1 spaghetti squash
2 tbsp butter
2 tbsp olive oil
4 cloves garlic - minced
1 shallot - chopped
A handful of parsley - Chopped
25 g Parmesan cheese - Grated
Pinch of salt
Pinch of pepper

Preparation:

1. Preheat the oven to 200°C.
2. Cut the pumpkin in half lengthways. Scoop out the seeds and discard.
3. Place the pumpkin cut side down on a deep baking tray lined with baking paper.
4. Drizzle with olive oil and season with salt and pepper.
5. Bake the pumpkin for 60 minutes.
6. Fry the shallots and garlic in a pan for 5 minutes.
7. Add the butter and parsley.
8. Remove the pumpkin flesh with a fork in the form of spaghetti strands and add to the pan.
9. Cook for 1-2 minutes.
10. Remove the pan from the heat and add the grated cheese.
11. Garnish with more parsley and Parmesan.

Wild rice with kidney beans

Servings: 5
Preparation time: 40 minutes
Do not prepare dish until 3-4 weeks of diet!

Ingredients:

250 g kidney beans, dried
2 garlic cloves
1 celery stalk, chopped
1 pepper, chopped
1 onion, diced
1 pinch of pepper
1.1 kg wild rice
800 ml water
1 bay leaf
¼ tsp thyme
1 pinch of salt

Preparation:

1. Put all the ingredients except the rice in the pressure cooker and mix well.
2. Close the lid and cook at high pressure for 25 minutes.
3. In the meantime, cook the rice in a normal pot with water.
4. Release the pressure normally and open.
5. Remove the bay leaf and mix well.
6. Serve with the rice and enjoy.

Simple chickpeas

Servings: 2
Preparation time: 45 minutes

Ingredients:

200 g chickpeas
2 bay leaves
3 garlic cloves
1 litre of water

Preparation:

1. Put the chickpeas, bay leaf, garlic and water in a pressure cooker.
2. Close the lid and cook for 35 minutes. For food processors: Select bean function.
3. Release the pressure normally and open.
4. Serve warm and enjoy.

Garlic Parsnip Gratin with Cheese

Servings: 4
Preparation time: 30 minutes

Ingredients:

650 g parsnips, sliced
230 g mozzarella
225 g cream cheese
1 tbsp garlic powder
½ tbsp pepper
500 ml vegetable stock
3 cloves of garlic, crushed
2 tbsp olive oil

Preparation:

1. Put all the ingredients except the cheese in the pressure cooker.
2. Close the lid and cook at high pressure for 4 minutes.
3. Allow the pressure to release normally.
4. Open the lid and add the cheese. Simmer in the pot with the other ingredients for 5 minutes.
5. Serve.

Cabbage and lentil soup with sweet potatoes

Servings: 4
Preparation time: 30 minutes
Do not prepare dish until the 3-4th week of diet!

Ingredients:

2 heads of kale, shredded
200 g lentils
1 sweet potato, diced
1 bay leaf
1 litre vegetable stock
2 garlic cloves, crushed
1 onion, diced
2 carrots, chopped and peeled
1 pinch of salt

Preparation:

1. Place lentils, garlic, onions, carrots, sweet potatoes, bay leaf and vegetable stock in pressure cooker.
2. Cook for 20 minutes under high pressure.
3. Open with the cold water method.
4. Add cabbage and salt. Stir constantly for 3 minutes.
5. Serve and enjoy.

Butternut squash with apple sauce

Servings: 4
Preparation time: 20 minutes
Do not prepare dish until 3-4 weeks of diet!

Ingredients:

500 g butternut squash
2 apples, cored and in pieces (Granny Smith)
¼ teaspoon cinnamon
1 pinch of ginger
250 ml water
2 tbsp coconut oil
1 onion, diced
1 pinch of salt

Preparation:

1. Put water in the pressure cooker. Prepare the steamer tray.
2. Place the apples, onion and pumpkin in the steamer.
3. Sprinkle with salt.
4. Close the lid and cook at high pressure for 8 minutes.
5. Open with the cold water method.
6. Place the apple-pumpkin mixture in a bowl. Mash with a masher.
7. Add the remaining ingredients and mix well.
8. Serve and enjoy.

Apple-Coconut Magic

Servings: 5

Preparation time: 15 minutes

Do not prepare dish until 3-4 weeks of diet!

Ingredients:

2 apples, peeled and diced (Granny Smith)

1 tbsp coconut oil

1 tsp cinnamon powder

2 tbsp. chia seeds

Stevia to sweeten as needed

2 tbsp cocoa powder

1 tbsp barley grass (from the health food store)

Preparation:

1. Put apple, cinnamon, coconut oil and lemon juice in a small saucepan.
2. Cook the mixture over medium heat for a few minutes until soft.
3. Sweeten with stevia as needed. Serve as a side dish with pudding or porridge. Enjoy.

Coconut Macaron

Servings: 1 baking tray
Preparation time: 25 minutes

Ingredients:

200 g coconut butter
60 g grated coconut
4 drops stevia
1 tsp vanilla
1 pinch of cinnamon
1 pinch nutmeg

Preparation:

1. Preheat oven to 160 degrees. Heat the coconut butter over a low heat, stirring constantly, until melted.
2. Mix the ingredients well in a bowl. If necessary, add a little more shredded coconut for a thicker consistency.
3. Form small biscuits and place on a baking tray.
4. Bake for 15 minutes. If necessary, remove from the oven earlier if the biscuits threaten to burn. Leave to cool and serve.

Quinoa gazpacho

Servings: 2
Preparation time: 20 minutes
Do not prepare dish until the 3-4th week of the diet!

Ingredients:

4 cucumbers, peeled
6 tomatoes
80 g quinoa, cooked
2 tbsp olive oil
1 pinch of salt
1 pinch of pepper
2 cloves garlic
1 pinch oregano
1 pinch black pepper

Preparation:

1. Juice the tomatoes, cucumber and garlic cloves in a juicer. Add the remaining ingredients to the finished juice mixture and mix well. Enjoy cold.
2. Optional: Simmer with 100-200 ml water over medium heat and enjoy hot.

Quinoa salad with cucumber

Servings: 2
Preparation time: 15 minutes
Do not prepare dish until 3-4 weeks of diet!

Ingredients:

170 g quinoa, cooked
1 clove garlic, crushed
1 cucumber, sliced
A handful of arugula leaves
1 red paprika, chopped
1 avocado, diced
2 tbsp chia seeds
2 tbsp olive oil
2 tbsp coconut milk
1 pinch of salt
1 pinch of pepper
Juice of one lemon

Preparation:

1. Put the ingredients in a salad bowl and mix well.
2. Drizzle with olive oil, coconut milk and lemon juice.
3. Enjoy.

Quinoa-Almond Smoothie with Algae

Servings: 2
Preparation time: 10 minutes

Ingredients:

170 g cooked quinoa, cooled down
Wakame (approx. 7-8 cm), soaked in water for approx. 10 minutes
500 ml almond milk
Juice of 2 lemons
4 carrots, peeled and sliced
A few sultanas to garnish
60 g kale

Preparation:

1. Puree all ingredients with a blender.
2. Garnish with a few sultanas. You can also puree them if you want a sweeter smoothie.

Quinoa pancakes

Servings: 6
Preparation time: 55 minutes

Ingredients:

170 g quinoa
40 g oats
500 ml coconut milk
120 g ground coconut
2 teaspoons almond essence
A little coconut oil or olive oil
2 tablespoons flaxseed
1 teaspoon salt
A few strawberries cut into strips for decoration (starting from the third week of the diet)

Preparation:

1. Mix the oats, flax seeds, together with the coconut and quinoa, in a food processor.
2. Mix the ground ingredients with almond essence/milk in a bowl. Leave to rest for 10 minutes.
3. Heat oil in a pot or pan.
4. Add some of the pound cake mixture to the pot and cook for 30-40 minutes on each side, on medium heat.
5. Decorate pancakes with strawberries.
6. Serve and enjoy.

Aubergine sandwich with chilli

Servings: 1
Preparation time: 10 minutes
Do not prepare dish until 3-4 weeks of diet!

Ingredients:

1 large aubergine, smoked
1 diced onion
1 finely chopped green chilli pepper
1 tomato, sliced
1 clove of garlic, crushed
½ teaspoon salt
A few chopped coriander leaves
1 teaspoon olive oil
¼ teaspoon pepper
Wholemeal sandwich or roll respectively

Preparation:

1. Mash the aubergine in a bowl with a spoon.
2. Add remaining ingredients except tomatoes and mix well. Use as sandwich filling.
3. Place tomato slices on top of the filling.

Smoked salmon frittata

Servings: 2
Preparation time: 15 minutes

Ingredients:

6 eggs
120 g smoked salmon
1 tsp/15 g butter
2 tbsp coriander, ground
1 pinch of pepper

Preparation:

1. Whisk eggs and pepper in a bowl.
2. Brush the bottom of the cooker with butter. Pour the whisked mixture into the rice cooker. Add salmon and spices on top.
3. Close the lid and cook for five minutes.
4. Done.

Fillet of beef breast with coconut butter

Servings: 6
Preparation time: 3 hours 30 minutes
Do not prepare dish until 3-4 weeks of diet!

Ingredients:

1.5 kg beef breast fillet
2 heaped teaspoons onion soup seasoning (mix a little garlic, cumin, thyme and a meat stock cube for this)
110 g coconut butter
30 g Dijon mustard

Preparation:

1. Preheat the oven to 150°C.
2. Place the beef brisket in a pan or baking dish (fat side up).
3. Mix the soup seasoning, coconut butter and mustard in a bowl.
4. Then spread the mixture evenly over the meat.
5. Cover the pan or baking dish with a lid or aluminium foil.
6. Bake in the oven for 3-4 hours.

Catfish soup with coconut and ginger

Servings: 2
Preparation time: 25 minutes

Ingredients:

220 g catfish - chopped into 2 cm pieces, boned
500 ml fish stock
250 ml coconut milk
1 tbsp lemongrass - thinly sliced
1 tbsp coriander leaves
1 tbsp Thai chillies - thinly sliced
1 tbsp galangal/Thai ginger - thinly sliced
1 clove garlic - crushed
4 tbsp fish sauce without additives
4 tbsp lime or lemon juice

Preparation:

1. Combine all ingredients except the fish and coconut milk in a soup pot.
2. Bring to the boil for at least 1 minute.
3. Reduce heat and simmer on low for 5 minutes.
4. Add the coconut milk and the fish.
5. Simmer for 10 minutes.

Oatmeal Quinoa Muesli

Servings: 1
Preparation time: 15 minutes
Do not prepare dish until the 3-4th week of the diet!

Ingredients:

200 g oat flakes
340 g quinoa flakes
140 g almonds, ground
40 g amaranth, puffed
140 g mulberries
150 g pumpkin seeds
125 g walnuts, chopped
150 g golden raisins/sultanas
60 g goji berries
95 g dried apricots, chopped
110 g dried sour cherries
40 g unsweetened and dried coconut flakes
75 g hemp seeds
75 g sunflower seeds
1 tablespoon ground cinnamon
1 teaspoon vanilla extract
A pinch of nutmeg
A pinch of sea salt

Preparation:

1. Mix all ingredients well in a large bowl.
2. Store in an airtight container.
3. Serve with almond milk, for example.

Slow Cooker Chicken

Servings: 2
Preparation time: 3 hours
Do not prepare dish until 3-4 weeks of diet!

Ingredients:

1 teaspoon dried oregano
½ teaspoon salt
¼ teaspoon pepper
1 kg chicken breast
2 tablespoons butter
120 ml chicken stock
120 ml white wine
90 ml fresh lemon juice
2 cloves garlic - chopped
1 teaspoon chicken stock - grained
½ teaspoon parsley

Preparation:

1. Mix all the spices in a pan. Bring to the boil.
2. Pour it over the chicken in the cooker.
3. Simmer on low for 3 hours.

Tacos from the slow cooker

Servings: 8
Preparation time: 5 hours
Do not prepare dish until the 3-4th week of the diet!

Ingredients:

1.5 kg beef; cut into small pieces
1 large onion; diced
4 cloves of garlic; minced
1 to 3 tbsp. chopped, smoked paprika
1 tsp oregano
2 bay leaves
A pinch of coarse-grained salt
400 g cabbage; cut into thin slices
10 radishes (halved and thinly sliced)
15 g fresh coriander
2 tbsp lime juice
Wholemeal tortillas
Topping: sour cream, salsa, jalapeno (thinly sliced), grated cheese
Coleslaw of your choice

Preparation:

1. In a slow cooker, combine beef, garlic, onions, smoked paprika, oregano, bay leaves and salt. (Tip: Add a little water to the bottom to prevent sticking).
2. Cook on high for 3.5 to 4 hours or on low for 7 to 8 hours.
3. Twenty minutes before the meat mixture is ready, wrap the tortillas in foil and heat in a preheated oven (180°C) for 5 to 10 minutes.
4. While the tortillas are heating up and the meat is getting ready, toss together the cabbage, radishes, lime juice and ¼ tsp salt.
5. Place the meat in a bowl and shred with a fork; keep the broth. Then slowly pour the broth over the meat and mix.
6. Fill tortillas with beef and coleslaw and top with toppings of choice.

Coconut chicken with teriyaki sauce

Servings: 4

Preparation time: 15 minutes + preparation overnight

Ingredients:

4 chicken breasts - boneless, skinless

1 bottle of teriyaki sauce without additives

1 tbsp coconut oil

420 g cooked rice (wholemeal)

Preparation:

1. Place the chicken in a large zipper storage bag.
2. Put half of the teriyaki sauce on the chicken.
3. Squeeze out as much air as possible and close the bag.
4. Shake the chicken to make sure it is well marinated. Refrigerate for 6-8 hours.
5. Put the oil in a medium frying pan over a medium heat.
6. Place the chicken in the pan, turning frequently. Cook until tender. This takes 8-10 minutes to prepare.
7. Add more teriyaki sauce, leaving some for serving.
8. Stir well to make sure the sauce gets everywhere, then serve on top of the rice.
9. Add the remaining teriyaki sauce as a small dip.

Steamed Asparagus

Servings: 4
Preparation time: 10 minutes

Ingredients:

500 g asparagus, peeled
1 tbsp onion powder
2 tbsp extra virgin olive oil
250 ml water
1 pinch of pepper
1 pinch of salt

Preparation:

1. Put water in the saucepan. Place the steamer insert in the pressure cooker.
2. Put the asparagus in and drizzle with olive oil.
3. Add the onion powder.
4. Close the lid and steam for 2-5 minutes.
5. Open with the cold water method.
6. Season with salt and pepper.
7. Serve.

Steamed Brussels sprouts with pine nuts

Servings: 4

Preparation time: 10 minutes

Ingredients:

500 g Brussels sprouts
4 tbsp pine nuts
250 ml water
A dash of olive oil
1 pinch of pepper
1 pinch of salt

Preparation:

1. Put water in the pressure cooker.
2. Add the Brussels sprouts in the steamer.
3. Close the lid and cook for 3 minutes under high pressure.
4. Open with the cold water method.
5. Season with salt, pepper and olive oil.
6. Sprinkle with pine nuts and serve.

Peas and whole grain rice

Servings: 2
Preparation time: 25 minutes

Ingredients:

110 g whole grain rice
75 g peas
500 ml vegetable stock without additives
2 tbsp butter
1 onion, diced
25 g Parmesan cheese
1 pinch of pepper

Preparation:

1. Sauté 3/2 tbsp butter in a pressure cooker.
2. When the butter has melted, add the onion and sauté until translucent.
3. Add the rice and stir until lightly browned.
4. Add the peas and vegetable stock. Stir well.
5. Close the lid and cook at high pressure for 8 minutes.
6. Let the pressure escape normally.
7. Add the remaining butter, pepper and Parmesan.
8. Wait one minute to allow the cheese and butter to melt.
9. Stir through and serve.

Wholemeal rice risotto

Servings: 4
Preparation time: 15 minutes

Ingredients:

225 g whole grain rice
90 g corn
75 g peas
1 red bell pepper, diced
750 ml vegetable stock without additives
1 tbsp extra virgin olive oil
2 cloves garlic, crushed
1 onion, diced
1 tsp spice mix
1 pinch of pepper
1 pinch of salt

Preparation:

1. Put olive oil in pressure cooker and heat.
2. When it is hot, sauté the onions and garlic for 4 minutes.
3. Add the rice and mix well.
4. As soon as it forms a uniform mass, add the rest of the ingredients and mix thoroughly.
5. Close the lid and cook for 8 minutes at high pressure.
6. Open with the cold water method.
7. Stir through and serve.

Sweet potato curry

Servings: 20
Preparation time: 25 minutes

Ingredients:

200 g chickpeas, cooked and drained
2 tbsp olive oil
4 sweet potatoes, diced
1 onion, diced
1 tbsp ginger powder
1 tbsp curry powder
120 ml vegetable stock
200 ml coconut milk
1 pinch salt
1 pinch of pepper
A handful of mint leaves
A little spinach as a garnish

Preparation:

1. Sauté the onions in 1 tbsp olive oil. Add the ginger, garlic, curry powder and salt.
2. Simmer for 2 minutes. Add potatoes and vegetable stock. Stir constantly.
3. When the potatoes are soft, add the coconut milk and chickpeas. Stir. Once the potatoes are cooked through, remove from the heat and serve garnished with mint leaves. Serve with a side dish of your choice, if desired.

Spinach Mint Smoothie

Servings: 1
Preparation time: 10 minutes

Ingredients:

150 g spinach, chopped
250 ml almond milk
2 tbsp mint, chopped
1 tsp stevia
A piece of lemon or a few mint leaves for garnish

Preparation:

1. Blend the almond milk and spinach in a blender.
2. When the mixture is uniform, add the rest of the ingredients.
3. Blend again until the mixture is uniform. Pour into a glass and enjoy.

Chicken coconut soup

Servings: 3
Preparation time: 40 minutes
Do not prepare dish until 3-4 weeks of diet!

Ingredients:

1 litre chicken stock
3 kaffir lime leaves
2 Thai chillies; small, halved lengthwise
2 garlic cloves; crushed
8 cm piece of ginger; fresh, peeled and cut into 4 pieces
1 stalk of lemongrass; only the light part, cracked with a knife
200 g chicken
400 ml coconut milk; unsweetened
240 g straw mushrooms (from a can); washed
2 tablespoons Thai fish sauce without additives
1 ½ teaspoons stevia as a sugar substitute
juice of 4 limes
pinch of salt
Pepper
15 g fresh coriander; chopped

Preparation:

1. Bring the chicken stock to the boil over medium heat using a soup pot.
2. Add the lime leaves, garlic, chillies, ginger and lemongrass.
3. Cover the pot and simmer over a medium-low heat for 10 minutes.
4. Stir in the chicken, mushrooms, coconut milk, stevia, lime juice and fish sauce.
5. Let everything simmer for another 5 minutes.
6. Now add a little salt and pepper.
7. Ladle the soup into a soup bowl and garnish with coriander.
8. Put the vegetables and chicken into a large soup pot over medium heat.
9. Pour about 3 litres of cold water into the pot.
10. Add the thyme, peppercorns and bay leaves. Bring it to the boil over medium-low heat.
11. As soon as it boils, remove the ingredients that rise to the surface from the water. Add water as needed.
12. Take out the chicken and place it on a cutting board until it is cool enough to touch. Remove the skin as well as the bones and cut the chicken into small pieces.
13. Pass the stock through a fine sieve and catch it in another pot.
14. Then add the vegetables to the pot with the strained broth.
15. Mix all the ingredients (except those removed during rising) and serve.

Amaranth Coconut Porridge

Servings: 2
Preparation time: 25 minutes

Ingredients:

500 ml water
200 g amaranth seeds
250 ml coconut milk
30 g coconut pieces

Preparation:

1. Add the amaranth to the boiling water.
2. Then simmer for 15-20 minutes.
3. Remove from the heat and add the remaining ingredients.
4. Mix well and enjoy.

Pumpkin soup with apple from the pressure cooker

Servings: 6

Preparation time: 25 minutes

Do not prepare dish until 3-4 weeks of diet!

Ingredients:

500 g butternut squash, peeled and diced

1 tablespoon olive oil

1 litre vegetable stock

1 tsp ginger powder

1 apple (variety: Granny Smith), peeled and sliced

Preparation:

1. Put olive oil in pressure cooker and sauté.
2. When the oil is hot, add the pumpkin and sauté for 5 minutes.
3. Add the rest of the ingredients and stir well.
4. Close the lid and cook for 10 minutes at high pressure.
5. Open with the cold water method.
6. Puree the soup.
7. Serve warm and enjoy.

Cucumber-carrot-celeriac salad

Servings: 2-4
Preparation time: 15 minutes
Do not prepare dish until 3-4 weeks of diet!

Ingredients:

1 apple (variety: Granny Smith), peeled and diced
2 tablespoons mayonnaise (sugar-free is essential!)
1 celeriac, peeled and grated
4 tbsp almonds, halved
Juice of one lemon
2 carrots, sliced
2 cucumbers, sliced
2 tbsp Cream of Coconut (coconut milk with thickened coconut fat)
A handful of parsley
1 tbsp olive oil
1 pinch of salt
1 pinch of pepper

Preparation:

1. Mix the ingredients together in a salad bowl.
2. Drizzle with mayonnaise and mix again.
3. Add olive oil and lemon juice. Season with salt and pepper.
4. Enjoy.

Artichoke Soy Salad

Servings: 2
Preparation time: 15 minutes

Ingredients:

2 artichoke hearts, halved, pickled in brine
A handful of arugula leaves
100 ml almond powder (ground almonds WITHOUT additives)
1 onion, diced
50 g bean sprouts

Dressing:

3 tbsp mayonnaise (sugar-free)
2 tbsp olive oil
Juice of one lemon

Preparation:

1. Mix ingredients in a salad bowl.
2. Add the mayonnaise. Mix again.
3. Drizzle with olive oil and lemon juice.
4. Enjoy.

Alfalfa Avocado Smoothie

Servings: 2
Preparation time: 10 minutes

Ingredients:

500 ml almond milk
50 g bean sprouts
50 g alfalfa sprouts
1 tsp ginger
½ avocado
1 apple
1 tbsp coconut oil

Preparation:

1. Blend almond milk, sprouts, avocado and apple in a blender.
2. Add the coconut oil and ginger.
3. Serve and enjoy.

Courgette and avocado vegetable pasta

Servings: 2
Preparation time: 40 minutes

Ingredients:

5 small courgettes
3 avocados
4 fresh basil leaves - chopped
1 tsp sea salt
3 tsp garlic powder
3 tbsp extra virgin olive oil
½ lemon
2 tbsp coconut oil
2 tsp onion powder
3 strips of fried bacon - chopped

Preparation:

1. Cut the courgettes into noodles or spiralise them with a spiral slicer, respectively.
2. Put the courgettes in a sieve. Add sea salt.
3. Leave to rest for 20 minutes.
4. Place the courgette noodles in a cloth or paper towels and squeeze them gently. Set aside.
5. Put the avocados, 1 tsp sea salt, basil, olive oil, garlic and lemon juice in a food processor/blender and blend until homogeneous.
6. Heat the coconut oil in a frying pan over a medium heat.
7. Add the courgette noodles and the onion and sauté for 2-3 minutes.
8. Add the avocado sauce and stir well.
9. Add the bacon pieces.
10. Serve and enjoy.

Apple and Avocado Soup with Arugula

Servings: 2
Preparation time: 15 minutes
Do not prepare dish until 3-4 weeks of diet!

Ingredients:

2 avocados, chopped
4 apples, chopped (variety: Granny Smith)
2 tablespoons white onions, chopped
A handful of arugula leaves
4 tablespoons extra virgin olive oil
1 litre of water
2-4 more tablespoons white onions, chopped, for garnish
1 pinch of salt
1 pinch of pepper
1 pinch of red pepper flakes

Preparation:

1. Chop the arugula. Prepare the remaining ingredients as indicated.
2. Blend avocado, apples, onions, ½ of the arugula and olive oil in a blender. Blend until a nice, uniform mixture is formed.
3. Season with salt and spices and garnish with arugula.
4. Serve garnished with pieces of onion.

Wholemeal pasta with candida-friendly sauce

Servings: 2
Preparation time: 50 minutes

Ingredients:

Vegetables:

¼ broccoli head, cut into approx. 2 cm florets
½ red bell pepper, cut into approx. 1 cm pieces
¼ yellow onion, thinly sliced into rings
2 teaspoons olive oil
Juice of half a lime
Pinch of salt

Sauce:

1 avocado, peeled and diced
Juice of half a lime
1 clove garlic, crushed
2 tablespoons coriander
Salt and pepper

Pasta:

150 g wholemeal pasta
A pinch of salt

Preparation:

1. Preheat oven to 230°C. Mix the broccoli, bell peppers and onions in a bowl. Add the olive oil, lime juice and a pinch of salt. Mix everything together and then spread as evenly as possible on a baking tray (with baking paper).
2. Roast the vegetables in the oven for 30 minutes, stirring 1-2 times. Remove from the oven and leave to cool slightly.
3. Bring a large pot of water with a pinch of salt to the boil. Stir in the penne. Cook pasta; stirring occasionally. Should be well al dente after about 11 minutes. Drain.
4. Blend avocado, lime juice, garlic and salt and pepper in a blender. Add the coriander and blend again briefly.
5. Arrange the noodles with the vegetables and sauce on a plate and enjoy.

Aubergine roll

Servings: 2
Preparation time: 10 minutes
Do not prepare dish until 3-4 weeks of diet!

Ingredients:

1 large aubergine, cut into thin slices
2 tomatoes, sliced
1 onion, cut into thin rings
4-5 lettuce leaves
3-4 basil leaves
½ teaspoon pepper
¼ teaspoon thyme
¼ teaspoon salt
1 tablespoon mayonnaise, sugar-free
1 clove of garlic, crushed
1 tablespoon olive oil
2 (burger) buns (wholemeal)

Preparation:

1. Sauté garlic with olive oil in a pan for 3 minutes. Add the aubergine pieces and fry until lightly browned on both sides.
2. Spread mayonnaise on burger buns. Top with lettuce leaves. Layer aubergines, onions and tomatoes on top. Sprinkle with pepper, thyme and salt.
3. Serve with a little barbecue sauce (optional).

Asparagus-Chinese cabbage magic from the wok

Servings: 5
Preparation time: 35 minutes
Do not prepare dish until 3-4 weeks of diet!

Ingredients:

90 ml olive oil
1 medium aubergine, diced
1 onion, diced
150 g asparagus, cut into 2 cm pieces
6 Chinese cabbage leaves
1 pinch oregano
1 pinch sage
1 pinch thyme
1 pinch of salt
1 pinch of pepper
A handful of croutons

Preparation:

1. Sauté the aubergine and onion in a hot wok for four minutes.
2. Add the asparagus and cabbage. Sauté for another four minutes.
3. Add the tomatoes, sage, oregano, salt, pepper and thyme.
4. Cover and simmer on low heat for 10-15 minutes.
5. Garnish the finished dish with croutons and serve.

Steamed cauliflower

Servings: 4
Preparation time: 25 minutes

Ingredients:

250 ml water
500 g cauliflower
Juice of one lemon
4 tbsp coriander, ground
1 pinch paprika powder
¼ tsp turmeric, ground
¼ tsp cumin
½ tbsp parsley
2 tbsp olive oil
1 pinch salt

Preparation:

1. Wash the cauliflower and cut into individual florets.
2. Place the florets in the steamer basket. Add water to the pressure cooker.
3. Close the lid and boil for one minute.
4. Open with the cold water method.
5. Set the cauliflower aside on a plate. Remove the water from the pot.
6. Add olive oil to pot and heat. Mash the cauliflower alongside.
7. When the oil is hot, add the cauliflower and sauté for a minute.
8. Add the rest of the ingredients. Sauté for two minutes, stirring constantly.
9. Add lemon juice to the cauliflower rice and serve.

Teriyaki salmon with ginger and stevia

Servings: 2
Preparation time: 30 minutes

Ingredients:

2 salmon fillets
2 tbsp coconut aminos or soy sauce
1 tbsp stevia
1 lemon
1 tbsp extra virgin olive oil
1 tbsp ginger - finely chopped

Preparation:

1. Mix all the ingredients together to make a marinade, except for the salmon.
2. Place the fillets in a baking dish and cover with the marinade.
3. Pour the mixture over the fish several times and cover with foil.
4. Bake in a preheated oven at 180°C for 20 minutes.

Halibut with rice

Servings: 6
Preparation time: 40 minutes

Ingredients:

2 teaspoons vegetable oil
4 shallots; finely chopped
2 ½ teaspoons red curry paste
500 ml chicken stock
130 ml coconut milk; light
½ teaspoon salt
pinch of salt
4x 120 g halibut fillets; without skin
1 kg spinach; sautéed
25 g coriander; chopped
2 spring onions; thinly sliced
2 tablespoons lime juice
Black pepper
500 g whole grain rice; cooked

Preparation:

1. Cook the rice according to the packet instructions.
2. Sauté the fresh spinach for 2 minutes in the microwave or steamer.
3. Heat the olive oil in a large frying pan over medium heat.
4. Add the onions and fry until brown. Stir occasionally.
5. Add the curry paste and cook for 30 seconds.
6. Now add the chicken stock, ½ teaspoon salt and the coconut milk and simmer for about 5 minutes until the liquid has reduced to about 0.5 litres.
7. Season the halibut with a pinch of salt.
8. Place the fish in the pan.
9. Shake the pan gently so that the fish is completely covered with the sauce.
10. Cover the pan and cook the halibut for about 7 minutes, until the fish can be easily torn with a fork.
11. Put the spinach on a soup plate.
12. Place the fish fillets on top of the spinach.
13. Stir the coriander and lime juice into the sauce.
14. Pour the sauce over the fish and serve with rice.

Tuna and courgette casserole

Servings: 3
Preparation time: 1 hour

Ingredients:

2 cans of tuna (approx. 150-200 g)
2 medium courgettes - Cut into spirals
1 small onion - Chopped
3 cloves garlic - Chopped
1 stick of celery - Chopped
3 tbsp ghee - divided into 1 tbsp and 2 tbsp
1 tbsp arrowroot powder
350 ml almond milk
salt
Pepper

Preparation:

1. Preheat the oven to 180°C.
2. Spiralise the courgettes.
3. Fry the onion, celery, garlic and 1 tbsp ghee, salt and pepper until the vegetables are golden brown.
4. Mix the 2 tbsp ghee with one tbsp arrowroot powder over medium heat until it is creamy and bubbling.
5. Add salt and pepper to taste.
6. Stir the almond milk until it is creamy and bubbling.
7. Mash the tuna with a fork and stir into the vegetables. Add the tuna mixture to the dish.
8. Spread the ghee mixture on top and bake for 45 minutes.

Crab from the wok

Servings: 6
Preparation time: 30 minutes
Do not prepare dish until 3-4 weeks of diet!

Ingredients:

350 ml fish stock
50 ml dark soy sauce
2 tbsp lemon juice
120 ml sherry
60 g black beans
80 g cashew
A handful of coriander leaves
One pound crab meat
1 tbsp carob bean gum as a corn starch substitute, mixed with 2 tbsp water
60 ml peanut oil
5 cloves garlic, crushed
1 tsp ginger, crushed
1 chilli pepper
4 edible crabs, chopped and cleaned
6 pak choi heads, halved and sautéed

Preparation:

1. Put fish stock, lemon juice, soy, sherry, cashews, beans and coriander in a pot.
2. Simmer for 5 minutes.
3. Add the crabmeat and cornflour (mixed with water). Increase heat and boil for one minute.
4. Meanwhile, heat peanut oil in a wok.
5. Add the ginger, garlic, crab pieces and chilli to the wok. Fry for 4 minutes.
6. Finally, mix the wok and saucepan contents and garnish with pak choi.
7. Enjoy.

Rice noodles and bean sprouts with shrimps

Servings: 4
Preparation time: 50 minutes
Do not prepare dish until the 3-4th week of the diet!

Ingredients:

240 g Thai rice noodles
60 ml fish sauce
50 g stevia as a sugar substitute
2 tbsp chilli sauce
2 tbsp lemon juice
60 ml vegetable oil
1 pound shrimps, butterfly cut (cut like a Wiener schnitzel)
4 cloves garlic, minced
1 block of tofu (approx. 200 g), cut into small pieces
6 radishes, chopped
4 spring onions, chopped
A handful of peanuts, roasted and salted (approx. 70 g)
200 g bean sprouts
2 jalapenos, chopped

Preparation:

1. Soak noodles in a bowl of warm water for 10 minutes.
2. Mix the fish sauce, chilli sauce, stevia and lemon juice in another bowl.
3. Drain the noodles.
4. Heat the wok.
5. Add vegetable oil and shrimps to wok. Fry hot for 2 minutes.
6. Transfer the shrimps to a bowl with a slotted spoon.
7. Leave the oil in the wok.
8. Fry the garlic and tofu in the wok until golden brown.
9. Add the noodles and a little fish sauce. Fry until the noodles have absorbed the fish sauce. Preparation time approx. 3 minutes. Add a little water if necessary so that the noodles do not dry out.
10. Add the spring onions, radishes and peanuts. Mix well.
11. Add the fish sauce mixture from the bowl and stir in. Heat the shrimp again in the wok for 2 minutes.
12. Arrange everything on a plate and garnish with bean sprouts and jalapeno pieces.
13. Enjoy.

Squid rings

Servings: 4
Preparation time: 30 minutes
Do not prepare dish until 3-4 weeks of diet!

Ingredients:

500 g rice noodles, cooked
60 ml coconut oil
500 g squid rings
150 g red onions, thinly sliced
½ tsp chopped chillies or chilli powder
2 garlic cloves, crushed
1 tbsp sherry or red wine vinegar
A handful of parsley, chopped

Preparation:

1. Cook rice noodles according to the instructions on the packet.
2. Melt the coconut oil in a large frying pan.
3. Sauté the onions in the pan and add the garlic. Sauté for 2-3 minutes. Stir well so that the onions and garlic are completely mixed.
4. Add the squid and chillies. Sauté for 3-5 minutes. Be careful not to fry them too hot. If necessary, work with less heat for 2-4 minutes longer.
5. Add the sherry vinegar and parsley. Mix everything together again and serve.

Coconut-almond tilapia

Servings: 3
Preparation time: 45 minutes

Ingredients:

500 g tilapia fillets
35 g almonds, unsalted
20 g dried coconut flakes, unsweetened
A pinch of salt
A pinch of pepper
2 tablespoons olive oil
Half a handful of parsley
A pinch of garlic salt

Preparation:

1. Preheat the oven to 190°C.
2. Line a baking tray with baking paper.
3. Mix the coconut, almonds, parsley, pepper and salt.
4. Mix in a food processor until everything is well blended. It should feel like breadcrumbs in terms of consistency.
5. Place the tilapia on the baking tray.
6. Sprinkle with garlic salt.
7. Put the coconut mixture on the top of the fish.
8. Drizzle the fish with olive oil.
9. Bake for 20 minutes until the fish is nicely browned.

Mac & No-Cheese Candida-Style

Servings: 4
Preparation time: 1 hour 15 minutes
Prepare dish only from the 3-4th week of diet!

Ingredients:

75 g macaroni, raw, wholemeal
1 teaspoon extra virgin olive oil
2 tablespoons diced onion
1 clove of garlic, crushed
40 g cashew nuts
1 tablespoon lemon juice
80 ml water
Salt and pepper to taste
1 tablespoon extra-virgin olive oil
2 tablespoons roasted red peppers, drained
½ teaspoon garlic powder
½ teaspoon onion powder

Preparation:

1. Preheat oven to 180°C.
2. In a medium pot, bring water (with a pinch of salt) to the boil. Add the pasta and cook for 8-10 minutes. Drain and place in a small baking dish.
3. Heat the olive oil in a pot over medium heat. Stir in onions and garlic and sauté for 3-5 minutes until lightly browned. Then add to the pasta.
4. Using a blender, blend the cashews, lemon juice, water and a pinch of salt until uniform. Gradually add the olive oil, pepper, garlic powder and onion powder. Mix well with the pasta.
5. Bake in the oven for about 45 minutes - or until the top is lightly browned. Leave to cool for 10 minutes and then sprinkle with black pepper. Done.

Cheese Macaroni

Servings: 6
Preparation time: 1 hour 30 minutes

Ingredients:

240 g uncooked macaroni, wholemeal
150 g cashew nuts
1 onion, diced
1 tsp garlic powder
1 tsp onion powder
120 g roasted red bell pepper
90 ml lemon juice
1 tbsp vegetable oil
90 ml rapeseed oil
300 ml water
Salt to taste
1 tbsp carob bean gum as a flour substitute

Preparation:

1. Preheat the oven to 180°C.
2. Put the macaroni in a large pot filled with boiling salted water and cook for 8 to 10 minutes, or until al dente. Drain and place in a baking dish.
3. Heat the vegetable oil in a medium frying pan over a medium heat. Add the onions and cook until tender and lightly browned. Carefully mix with the macaroni.
4. Puree the cashews with the water, lemon juice and salt in a food processor. Mix in the rapeseed oil, red pepper, locust bean gum, onion powder and garlic powder.
5. Mix with the macaroni and onions and bake for about 45 minutes, or until lightly browned.
6. Leave the macaroni to cool for 10-15 minutes before serving.

Rice Cooker Noodle Soup with Peas and Olives

Servings: 2
Preparation time: 40 minutes
Do not prepare dish until 3-4 weeks of diet!

Ingredients:

1 tbsp olive oil
1 clove of garlic, crushed
1 onion, diced
3 carrots, chopped
400 g peas
450 g strained tomatoes
150 ml vegetable juice
60 ml water
3 tbsp red wine
2 tbsp Worcestershire sauce without additives or vegetable stock
200 g wholemeal Farfalle pasta
1 pinch of mixed spices of your choice
1 pinch salt/pepper

Preparation:

1. If technically necessary: preheat for 10 minutes with the steam cooking function. Otherwise, let the rice cooker heat up on standard settings.
2. Add the oil, onions and garlic. Sauté.
3. Add the remaining ingredients.
4. Cook for 25 minutes.
5. Serve.

Quick pressure cooker pasta

Servings: 6
Preparation time: 15 minutes

Ingredients:

500 g wholemeal pasta
1 cup coffee cream
450 g broccoli
450 g cheddar cheese, grated
1l water

Preparation:

1. Put the pasta, broccoli and water in the saucepan and mix well.
2. Cook for 4 minutes at high pressure.
3. Open with the cold water method.
4. Add cheese and coffee cream. Now slowly sauté and stir the contents of the saucepan until the cheese has melted completely.
5. Serve and enjoy.

Sweet & spicy spaghetti from the pressure cooker

Servings: 6
Preparation time: 15 minutes
Do not prepare dish until the 3-4th week of dieting!

Ingredients:

500 g wholemeal spaghetti
2 tsp basil
2 garlic cloves, crushed
1 onion, diced
2 tbsp olive oil
600 ml water
1 can tomatoes, strained
90 g tomato paste
800 g tomatoes, sliced
1 pinch of chilli
1 tsp stevia
2 tsp parsley
1 tsp oregano
1 pinch salt
1 pinch of pepper

Preparation:

1. Heat the olive oil in a pot.
2. When it is hot, add the onions and sauté for 2 minutes.
3. Add the garlic and sauté for one minute.
4. Add the rest of the ingredients and stir well.
5. Close the lid and cook at high pressure for 5 minutes.
6. Allow the pressure to release normally.
7. Stir through and serve.

Spelt spaghetti

Servings: 8
Preparation time: 30 minutes

Ingredients:

200 g spelt spaghetti
A handful of mushrooms, sliced
1 clove of garlic
2 onions, diced
200 g cream or oat cream
A pinch of herb salt
2 tablespoons sesame oil

Preparation:

1. First cook the spelt spaghetti according to the instructions and set aside.
2. Heat a little sesame oil in a pan to sauté the onions. Add the crushed garlic and fry.
3. Then add the sliced mushrooms and the herb salt.
4. Wait until the mushrooms are soft, then add the oat cream.
5. Add a handful of onions and herb salt.
6. Add a little freshly chopped parsley on top and serve with the spaghetti. Enjoy your meal!

Breakfast wrap with egg

Servings: 1
Preparation time: 15 minutes
Do not prepare dish until 3-4 weeks of diet!

Ingredients:

2 large eggs
1 small white onion, cut into thin rings
75 g mushrooms, halved
1 green pepper, sliced
Salt and pepper to taste
A pinch of chilli powder
1 teaspoon coconut milk
Olive oil (for frying)
A hot sauce of your choice
One wholemeal tortilla
A handful of grated cheese

Preparation:

1. Whisk one egg with all the spices in a bowl. Heat the oil in a pan and add the eggs.
2. Sprinkle with mushrooms, bell peppers and onions. Break the eggs with a spatula and mix well.
3. Do not use too much heat so that nothing burns. Fry the egg and vegetable mixture.
4. Drizzle with cheese and sauce. Put the finished mixture into the tortilla.

Quinoa Oat Goji Breakfast

Servings: 1
Preparation time: 15 minutes
Do not prepare dish until the 3-4th week of the diet!

Ingredients:

200 g oat flakes
340 g quinoa flakes
140 g almonds, ground
40 g amaranth, puffed
140 g mulberries
150 g pumpkin seeds
125 g walnuts, chopped
150 g golden raisins/sultanas
60 g goji berries
95 g dried apricots, chopped
110 g dried sour cherries
40 g unsweetened and dried coconut flakes
75 g hemp seeds
75 g sunflower seeds
1 tablespoon ground cinnamon
1 teaspoon vanilla extract
A pinch of nutmeg
A pinch of sea salt

Preparation:

1. Mix all ingredients well in a large bowl.
2. Store in an airtight container.
3. Serve in almond milk, for example.

Date muesli

Servings: 4
Preparation time: 40 minutes
Do not prepare dish until 3-4 weeks of diet!

Ingredients:

1 tsp. coconut oil
2 tbsp stevia powder
1 tsp ginger powder
1 tsp vanilla extract
170 g quinoa, cooked
½ tsp cinnamon
30 g almonds, soaked
30 g pumpkin seeds
30 g coconut, dried
30 g dates, dried
A little natural yoghurt

Preparation:

1. Preheat oven to 150 degrees.
2. Whisk together the coconut oil, stevia and vanilla extract to make a syrup. Mix the cinnamon and quinoa and spread evenly on the baking tray. Bake in the oven for 10 minutes.
3. Add the almonds, pumpkin seeds and desiccated coconut and spread evenly. Drizzle syrup over the top and spread evenly. Bake for a further 20 minutes.
4. Add the dried dates and leave to cool. Cut the cooled mixture into muesli bar pieces and enjoy.

Chickpea sandwich

Servings: 2
Preparation time: 15 minutes
Do not prepare dish until 3-4 weeks of diet!

Ingredients:

2 tomatoes, chopped
5 tablespoons chickpea flour
1 finely chopped green chilli pepper
½ teaspoon thyme leaves
¼ teaspoon turmeric
½ teaspoon salt
¼ teaspoon pepper powder
100 ml water
A few chopped coriander leaves
1 teaspoon oil
Sandwiches or rolls, wholemeal of course

Preparation:

1. In a bowl, mix all ingredients except oil and tomatoes.
2. Put oil in a pot and add half of the bowl mixture. Place the tomatoes on top and fry on both sides.
3. Use the resulting pancake as a sandwich filling.
4. Tomato chilli sauce is good as a small side dish.

Homemade bread with pumpkin

Servings: 8
Preparation time: 2-3 hours

Ingredients:

1 tbsp olive oil
2 tbsp linseed
2 tbsp warm water
350 g pumpkin puree
50 g stevia
3 tbsp coconut oil, melted
1 tbsp locust bean gum as a substitute for baking powder
1 tsp cinnamon
1 pinch nutmeg
1 pinch of salt
200 ml almond milk
250 g wholemeal flour
80 g oat flakes
Baking tin

Preparation:

1. Preheat oven to 180 degrees. Oil the baking tin with olive oil.
2. In a bowl, mix warm water with flax seeds. Leave to rest for 5 minutes.
3. In another bowl, mix together pumpkin puree, stevia, coconut oil, locust bean gum, cinnamon, nutmeg and salt.
4. Add the flaxseed mixture and almond milk. Mix well. Mix the flour together with the oat flakes. Add the flour mixture to the puree mixture and mix well.
5. Pour the finished mixture into a baking tin and bake for one hour. Leave to cool for half an hour and enjoy.

Courgette noodles with bacon

Servings: 2
Preparation time: 40 minutes
Do not prepare dish until 3-4 weeks of diet!

Ingredients:

500 g cherry tomatoes
6 strips of bacon - Cut into 2 cm pieces
A handful of basil leaves - Loosely packed
1 tbsp lard - melted
1 pinch of salt
Black pepper
3 medium courgettes
1 medium, ripe avocado

Preparation:

1. Bring a large pot full of water with salt to the boil. Meanwhile, preheat the oven to 180°C.
2. Mix the tomatoes, basil and bacon on a baking tray with the lard.
3. Sprinkle with the pepper and mix again.
4. Bake the tomatoes, basil and bacon for 20 minutes.
5. Cut off the ends of the courgettes and cut or spiralise them into courgette noodles.
6. Blanch the courgette noodles in the pot of boiling water for two minutes. Rinse the courgette noodles with cold water and then dry them with a towel. When the tomato mixture is ready, mix it with the courgette noodles and avocado.

Courgette fettuccine

Servings: 4
Preparation time: 1 hour 10 minutes

Ingredients:

1 medium butternut squash/musk squash/edible pumpkin
3 tbsp coconut oil - Separate
1 medium yellow onion - Chopped
2 cloves garlic - Minced
2 tsp rosemary - Dried
250 ml coconut milk
120 ml vegetable stock
½ tsp sea salt
500 g Mushrooms - Chopped
1.5 kg courgettes - Cut into spirals
Pepper to taste

Preparation:

1. Preheat the oven to 190°C.
2. Cut the pumpkin in half lengthways.
3. Grease a baking tray with 1 tbsp coconut oil and place the pumpkin on it, cut side down.
4. Roast for 30-45 minutes until soft.
5. Allow the pumpkin to cool.
6. Scoop out the pumpkin flesh and discard the skin.
7. Place the pumpkin (or pumpkin flesh) in a blender.
8. Place 1 tbsp coconut oil in a frying pan over a medium heat.
9. Add the onions and garlic. Fry both for 3-5 minutes.
10. Next, add the garlic and onions, coconut milk, rosemary, stock and salt to the pumpkin in the blender. Blend until smooth.
11. Put the remaining coconut oil in a pan. Add the mushrooms and sauté for 2 minutes. Add the courgettes and cook for 3 minutes.
12. Add the sauce to the pan and heat through.
13. Serve garnished with pepper.

Image sources/printing information
Cover: "Variety of Vegetables" | Ella Olsson | Pexels
BuchHoernchen-Verlag (Squirrel Books)
Im Schlimm 13
55768 Hoppstaedten-Weiersbach (Germany)
ISBN: 978-3-98500-345-7

Printed in Great Britain
by Amazon

62465102R00092